THE NEW TOWER
OF
BABEL

THE NEW TOWER OF BABEL

DR. JEAN MAALOUF

Dedication

I dedicate this book to:

Those who rightly replace Pilate's convenient and evasive question, "What is truth?" by the accurate and piercing question "Who is truth?"

Those who point to the "Who is truth" One boldly, fearlessly, and without compromise and complicity,

And those who are trusted guides in the times of the new Babel and the confusion of tongues.

"If there is no God, everything is permitted."
— Fyodor Dostoevsky

"When men choose not to believe in God, they do not thereafter believe in nothing, they then become capable of believing in anything."
— G.K. Chesterton

"In the beginning God created man in His own image, and man has been trying to repay the favor ever since."
— Voltaire

"I pray God to rid me of God.… The highest and loftiest thing that one can let go of is to let go of God for the sake of God."
— Meister Eckhart

"God is proved not only by the zeal of those who seek Him, but by the blindness of those who seek Him not."
— Blaise Pascal

"It is dangerous to talk glibly about the infinite God. It is sometimes dangerous to talk about Him at all, unless talking of Him brings you deeper into His mystery, and finally flattens you into silence in the face of His transcendence!"
— Thomas Merton

"There is enough light for those who desire to see, and enough obscurity for those who have a contrary disposition."
— Blaise Pascal

"Before God we are all equally wise and equally foolish."
— Albert Einstein

"We may ignore, but we can nowhere evade the presence of God. The world is crowded with Him. He walks everywhere incognito."
— C.S. Lewis

"I gave in, and admitted that God was God."
— C.S. Lewis

"Then Paul stood in front of the Areopagus and said, 'Athenians, I see how extremely religious you are in every way. For as I went through the city and looked carefully at the objects of your worship, I found among them an altar with the inscription, 'To an unknown god.' What therefore you worship as unknown, this I proclaim to you."
— Acts 17:22-23

Contents

Part Three: God's Substitutes

Introduction

The Tower of Babel—Then and Now

We no longer seem to speak the same "language" for we have chosen different gods, different values, different rules for life, different lifestyles, different measures for what is right and what is wrong, and different "truths" altogether.

The story of the Tower of Babel tells us that we have been there before. Our so-called new world order is not new at all. We have built the Tower of Babel very long ago, and we rebuilt it again and again throughout the centuries.

Although the circumstances have changed now, the essence of the story of the Tower is still the same. We might be in denial of its reality, but being in denial does not make the reality other than what it is.

Let us remember the Tower's story together as it was described in Genesis:

¹And the whole earth was of one language, and of one speech.

²And it came to pass, as they journeyed from the east, that they found a plain in the land of Shi'-nar; and they dwelt there.

³And they said one to another, Go to, let us make brick, and burn them thoroughly. And they had brick for stone, and slime had they for mortar.

⁴ And they said, Go to, let us build us a city and a tower, whose top may reach unto heaven; and let us make us a name, lest we be scattered abroad upon the face of the whole earth.

⁵ And the LORD came down to see the city and the tower, which the children of men builded.

⁶ And the LORD said, Behold, the people is one, and they have all one language; and this they begin to do: and now nothing will be restrained from them, which they have imagined to do.

⁷ Go to, let us go down, and there confound their language, that they may not understand one another's speech.

⁸ So the LORD scattered them abroad from thence upon the face of all the earth: and they left off to build the city.

⁹ Therefore is the name of it called Babel; because the LORD did there confound the language of all the earth: and from thence did the LORD scatter them abroad upon the face of all the earth. (Genesis 11:1-9 KJV)

The builders intended to build a tower into the heavens – a metaphor for the attempt to reach the infinite by the finite, and eventually replace the infinite by the finite or make the finite itself, infinite.

The people of Babel had big plans; they wanted to do something that was not done before and they wanted to do it by themselves without God. They were wealthy; they had the means to do it. They were prideful; they wanted to make a name for themselves. They were idolatrous; they wanted to ignore God and worship their "selves."

This was then. But, what about now? Aren't we doing the same thing?

We, too, intend to reach into the heavens, don't we?

Indeed, through our technology, social systems, and material achievements, we have created an edifice that reaches high, very high. The "bricks" of the Tower are our tremendous achievements, inventions, and successes. We have decoded the human genome and made huge discoveries in science, medicine, engineering, and practically in all other fields. We call this new reality the technological revolution, civilization, human achievement, progress, new creation or new genesis – a perfect world that speaks the high tech language. We now have translators and software that can allow for rapid communication with people of other languages, other traditions, and other ways of thinking and expressing themselves. Our language is the electronic language. With this language that reaches the furthest corner of the earth as well as the highest star in the skies, we intend to "make a name for ourselves" and worship "man" and his achievements instead of God. The tower of the new genesis seems even higher and more extended than the tower of the Genesis of the Old Testament.

But here is the problem. Even if we are closer to "the heavens," we don't seem satisfied and happier than before. If we are, why in the world are we killing each other for a futile reason or for no reason at all? Why do we hate each other? Why do we have more enemies than friends and why do we need to create enemies when we don't have them? Why do we use this electronic common language for spreading what hurts and destroys more than for spreading what heals and builds?

We may have solved some material problems and we feel better off in this regard, but the "heavens" remain just as far away as ever, especially when it comes to our relationships with others, with ourselves, and with God. Doesn't God's voice still reverberate throughout human history, now more than ever before, and ask Cain again and again, after Cain killed his brother Abel, "Where is your brother Abel?" (Genesis 4:9)

Cain was one person at that time of Genesis. Now, and since we are closer to the "heavens" with our so many incredible electronic achievements, we have the capacity to instantly exterminate thousands and millions of "Cains," and for what? To prove to ourselves that we are the masters of our destiny and that we do not need anyone – certainly not God – to tell us what to do?

Knowingly or unknowingly, we are re-living the story of The Tower of Babel in a new version.

There are several possible scenarios in store for our new Tower of Babel enterprise.

One scenario would be a total collapse of the tower because of the weakened foundation that can no longer bear the accumulated materialistic structure's weight. Many thinkers are starting to talk about such an eventuality predicting that our electronic civilization – our "tower of Babel" – will become another civilization whose end has come and will be added to the list of the several other civilizations that came and were gone in human history.

Another scenario would be an attempt to create a "global society" and a "World Community." *The Humanist Manifesto II* described it this way:

We deplore the division of humankind on nationalistic grounds. We have reached a turning point in human history where the best option is to transcend the limits of national sovereignty and to move toward the building of a world community in which all sectors of the human family can participate. Thus we look to the development of a system of world law and a world order based upon transnational federal government.

We find insufficient evidence for belief in the existence of a supernatural; it is either meaningless or irrelevant to the question of survival and fulfillment of the human race. As nontheists, we begin with humans not God, nature not deity. Nature may indeed be broader and deeper than we now know; any new discoveries, however, will but enlarge our knowledge of the natural.

But we can discover no divine purpose or providence for the human species. While there is much that we do not know, humans are responsible for what we are or will become. No deity will save us; we must save ourselves.

Indeed, many scientists are in open defiance of God. They plan for a world in which "man" is his own god and, in a concerted mass effort as was the case for the Tower of Babel of Genesis, they intend to accomplish such a purpose. Babel was also a symbol of a unifying plan against God; everything must be man-made and man-controlled. In this sense, cloning, for example, would be a tangible illustration of another intrusion into God's sovereignty by a "man making man after his own image" method.

Another scenario would be what some of us are trying to do: form a One World Government via means of global economy and by convincing people that separate nation states with their own laws, values, and borders are gone. Separate states bring "chaos" and chaos induces violence, and does not make good business. Therefore, a One World Government will control everything, will stop wars, will provide prosperity, and will make everyone happy.

We seem to be going this way, don't we? We already have created the EU (European Union), for example, the WTO (World Trade Organization), the NAFTA (North American Free Trade Agreement), and the many, many others organizations and agencies including the most famous one: the UN (United Nations). By the way, it can be said here that the first federation of people was not the United Nations or any other agency of recent times. The first federation of humans was that society that came together to build the Tower of Babel with the intention to exalt "man" and exclude God, to deify "man" and dethrone God, and to glorify "man" and despise God.

There is no doubt that any unification between organizations, agencies, or countries would sound like a good idea. Unity is good.

However, this unity becomes suspicious if its ultimate goal is just to make more money or have more power and control. The risk, then, would be to replace God and his laws with the new "more money," the new "more power," and the new "One World Order" that intends to replace the Maker.

The builders of the new Tower of Babel want to place humans above God, and the all powerful One World Government above all men and women. Doesn't this smell of tyranny? If "Power corrupts, and absolute power corrupts absolutely," as Lord Acton suggested, then corruption is to be expected, and our new "Tower of Babel" will absolutely fall too. If God is no longer in the picture and people turn their attention from him, and if they replace him with things of this world, God then will react as he did before. He will "confuse their language there, so that they will not understand one another's speech," as it was written in the story of the Tower of Babel. There are signs of the next wars – electronic wars. If some enemies succeed in inserting a powerful virus in our computers' systems, they will disrupt our communication systems and confuse our language so that we won't be able to "understand one another's speech." This happened before and it could happen again. Here too, it is true that "the more things change the more they stay the same," as an old French saying summarized it. A man-made world without including God in it is a utopian world – a delusion. Thus, the higher the tower is, the bigger the fall.

Still another scenario would be what the builders of the Genesis Tower of Babel did: they abandoned their attempt. The story says that the Babylonians woke up one day to find themselves speaking different languages. They could not understand each other. Therefore, there was no possibility for communication, consensus, and dialogue. Aren't we talking now about a possible "clash of civilizations" because we sometimes cannot find a common ground between us, we cannot have a genuine consensus, and we cannot maintain a true in-depth dialogue?

No wonder people feel the need to go back to nature and to the simple life that is lived more freely, more slowly, more mindfully, more authentically, more joyfully, and is more fulfilling. A shift of perception is needed. We might still build towers with our high tech and culture, but our motivation will be different because our perception will become different.

Woe to us all if one day we do not speak the same "language," and we stop understanding what the other is saying.

Unfortunately, we no longer seem to speak the same "language" for we have chosen different gods, different values, different rules for life, different lifestyles, different criteria and measures for what is right and what is wrong, and different truths altogether. But why and how did we get there? The book you are about to read will try to answer this question.

Part One

The Promethean Fire

1

The Promethean Fire

Our lives run on "fire." When it is not the flame of the Holy Spirit, this fire is a promethean fire.

The word "Promethean" refers to the Greek myth of Prometheus, whose gift of fire to humankind has come to symbolize knowledge, enlightenment, freedom, and resistance to authoritarian regimes and rules.

By itself, fire is a very powerful reality. We use fire to cook food, melt metals, provide warmth in cold winters, and just to survive. Fire is also a powerful symbol. It represents the start of civilization, restless energy, progressive technology, and bright future.

However, the problem emerges when such a fire is not contained to its territory, and goes free, ravaging other territories and reducing each and every one of them – dry or green – into ashes. Moreover, and this is worse, this fire may reach the source where it came from and deny its very existence. Consequently, and in such a case, Scripture will no longer be necessary, Revelation will no longer be recognized, and Tradition will no longer be allowed to dictate anything. Only "fire" will make sense by devouring any establishment.

According to the myth, this fire was stolen from the gods and given to humans in defiance of Zeus. So, if we come to exclude the divine – the very source of the fire – and we start to count solely on ourselves, pretending that we do not need anyone else to save us or make us happy, then we practically are self-referential and self-righteous. Here, the lines written by Pope Francis cannot but come to mind. He wrote:

> This worldliness can be fuelled in two deeply interrelated ways. One is the attraction of gnosticism, a purely subjective faith whose only interest is a certain experience or a set of ideas and bits of information which are meant to console and enlighten, but which ultimately keep one imprisoned in his or her own thoughts and feelings. The other is the self-absorbed promethean neopelagianism of those who ultimately trust only in their own powers and feel superior to others because they observe certain rules or remain intransigently faithful to a particular Catholic style from the past. A supposed soundness of doctrine or discipline leads instead to a narcissistic and authoritarian elitism, whereby instead of evangelizing, one analyzes and classifies others, and instead of opening the door to grace, one exhausts his or her energies in inspecting and verifying. In neither case is one really concerned about Jesus Christ or others. These are manifestations of an anthropocentric immanentism. It is impossible to think that a genuine evangelizing thrust could emerge from these adulterated forms of Christianity. (Apostolic Exhortation *EVANGELII GAUDEUM* [*Joy of the Gospel*], November 24, 2013, #94)

It is no wonder, then, that we are able to declare that we are our own masters and we are the ones who decide what is right and what is wrong.

We act as if we are self-help and self-creation individuals. We trust only in our own powers, we feel superior to others, and we redefine our own values according to our own interests, convenience, biases, and ideologies. We do this at the individual level under names such as self-esteem, self-help, and self-righteousness. We also do it at the collective level under names such as common good, patriotism, and self-preservation or survival.

We may play the appearance of being "perfect," when we are far from being perfect. We may be scrupulous about practicing our religion according to our denomination, and yet we find ourselves living the way of a "self-absorbed promethean neopelagianism" (excluding our dependence of God and the necessity of grace for salvation). We forget that it is God who saves us, and not some hypocritical observance of the rules and the performance of the good deeds.

Believing in the right doctrines according to the right formulas, and accomplishing the right actions according to the books and traditions as if God's grace is not necessary and has nothing to do with what we believe and do, will not guarantee us our salvation. Asceticism, good works, and personal discipline cannot achieve salvation by themselves. Prayer and all spiritual practices are not only important, but also critical. However, doing all these good things without counting on God's grace would be just a promethean neopelagianism of the pious. Pelagianism (denial of the original sin and the necessity of grace) was a heresy and it still is. It is, in blunt terms, a failure to accept the limits of being human.

Our contemporary culture is trying hard to convince us to adopt the promethean attitude which leads us to think that we are in control of our life, destiny, and death, and that we are the masters of our decisions counting solely on the wonders of our brains and technology.

The promethean fire is not only reason and skills, it is imagination that denies all restraints and excides all limits. We dream to be the god we are not by challenging the God that exists and declaring our independence from any divine order other than the one we imagine. We dream of the secular city that completely abandons the sacred in our daily life. We dream, as the promethean archetypal revolutionary suggests, of transforming our human condition from one that is dependent on outside forces to one that is the master of its own destiny.

In a sense, this is a good example that illustrates the "God is dead" of Nietzsche.

It is true that, throughout history and more particularly in modern times, Prometheus has symbolized, and is still symbolizing more than ever before, unyielding strength for great creativity, intellect, generosity, and boldness in the march toward an enlightened and productive world. But, it is also true, and in the same breath, that this same promethean fire has ignited a restless and uncontrollable energy for destruction and annihilation (weapons of mass destruction and continuous wars), instant anything (speed records, unmindful shortcuts, unconcerned quick fixes), and a weird and unheard of technology (cloning, creating laboratory babies, sending viruses that can destroy all electronic data).

Fyodor Dostoevsky had this insight: "If there is no God, everything is permitted." Doesn't this describe eloquently, in just eight words, the confusing situation of modern times?

The "Everything is permitted" may include the illusion of the ability to replace God. We do it when we convince ourselves that there are no limits to our "divine" ambition. Then, the original story of the biblical creation is bound to be repeated again and again; "You will not die," said the serpent to Adam and Eve, "for God knows that when you eat of it your eyes will be opened, and you will be like God, knowing good and evil" (Genesis 3:4). No doubt, this was the big lie that generated all other lies ever after.

By handing out the fire to humankind, Prometheus handed out the ability to be independent of God. The fire was meant to be for the progress and the betterment of humans, and it was supposed to logically add praises to the gods where it originally came from. But this did not happen and the myth said that Zeus was so angry that he punished Prometheus very severely by chaining him to a rock and having his liver eaten out every day by an eagle. Even though the story says that his liver would grow back every night, his punishment was meant to remain for eternity.

Yes, for the hope of a bright future and possibilities for growth and development at all levels of human existence, but no, for doing all this without any reference to where all these things come from. It is in our own interest to recognize where things belong because a promethean inflation that causes self-righteousness will unavoidably cause us big troubles. The painful collapse of the illusions of narcissism leads to apathy, listlessness, absurdity, and a sense of futility, and the meaninglessness of life. Then all human efforts and hopes seem as "Vanity of vanities! All is vanity" (Ecclesiastes 1:1).

Modern humans thought that by getting rid of God, they had freed themselves from all that repressed them. Instead they discovered that by killing God, they had also killed themselves by losing all that is meaningful in their lives. Then everything is permitted – a contradictory and destructive form of "self-creation."

In this sense, the promethean perspective, beside the fact that it is an anti-theistic theory, is an anti-humanistic prescription as well. On the one hand, it rejects the Infinite – God. On the other hand, it rejects the finite – human nature. In the name of being intensely human because it calls to realize the full human potential, it demands humans to go beyond their human nature and recreate themselves according to a pattern that is not human. When they realize that they failed because of their unattainable goals, they feel left with no place to find rest, no place to stand, and no reason to live for.

With God, the "fire" can produce wonders. Without God, the "fire" can reduce everything to ashes.

Only insane gods could invent weapons of mass destruction and use them against one another. Is destroying a city in order to save it a good reason for doing what we usually do in times of war?

Nothing is more dangerous than the illusion of being the gods we are not.

It should not shock us when the violence that we export through books, films, video games, weapons, and other means to foreign lands comes back with vengeance to our own lands. If "God is dead," Prometheus, sooner rather than later, will die also.

2

"If There Is No God, Everything Is Permitted"

If God does not exist, then everything becomes permissible. This is what Ivan Karamazov claims in Fyodor Dostoevsky's *The Brothers Karamazov.* He said: "If there is no God, everything is permitted," and everything becomes relative.

There are no rules to live by, no moral law to follow, no absolutes to light our paths, and no black and white truths to guide our journeys.

There are no systems more valid than others because there are no objective standards of truth. There are no solid references for anything. There are no revealed scriptures, no traditions, and no enforcing authoritative mechanisms. If there are some, they cannot be coercive by any means.

There are no valid moral codes that transcend space and time and that are universally recognized. All morals are relative to particular social groups. Each group decides its own ethics. Even each individual in the same group may insert a fitting personal conviction.

There are no "Ought-to-do-or-not-to-do" rules for action that fit all situations in time and space. Rights and wrongs are dependent upon this or that particular situation. Gone are the Ten Commandments. Gone are the general principles viewed as absolutes. Gone are the sub-principles arranged according to various patterns of behaviors and practical lifestyles. Now is the time of "situational ethics" that takes account of the particular situation, the distinctiveness, and the uniqueness of each person. Consequently, there are no "pre-fab" answers apart from the particular facts, situations, and contexts. Everything is right or wrong depending upon this or that particular situation.

No wonder some philosophers, like Jean-Paul Sartre, for example, have assumed that Ivan was right; if there was no God, who was to tell us what we ought to do or not do?

What could ethics be without God? For Sartre, the starting point of ethics is subjectivity, and not God. Existence comes first, not essence. A person exists, and then he or she makes choices. Human beings decide their own future. They must assume the great burden of responsibility for humanity by taking care of this humanity and by creating values and ethics. Humans have no excuses for doing so, and they act alone. Whatever humanity is, humans have created it.

Sartre wrote from an atheistic position in a post WWII Europe whose faith was shaken. That world was no longer a world where there was a solid faith in God, and where ethics seemed easier to know and practice – just consult the scripture texts and the official teachings of the Church in order to find out what the right choices are. With Sartre and the philosophers who thought like him, there were no longer such references. There were humans who created their own humanity as they pleased and continued to do so.

This kind of philosophy that celebrates existentialism, subjectivism, humanism, and relativism is pervasive in our culture today. It seems to deeply permeate almost every aspect of our lives, especially when it comes to our religious beliefs. More and more, we tend to pick and choose what is convenient to us in a large "cafeteria" of religions and spiritual traditions, and we disregard what is not convenient. Of course absolute truth is being abandoned since "there is no God," and with it the idea that there really is a right and wrong. Then, every fantasy is tolerated and accepted, and no one has the right to point the finger toward what used to be called a "sin" or at least a bad behavior. In other words, this is the "anything goes" philosophy that is taking over, and if anyone dares to say anything against it, he or she is labeled as an intolerant bigot.

But here is the problem. It is incredibly hypocritical and contradictory of those who profess that all opinions, points of view, and convictions are true, yet reject the opinions, points of view, and convictions of those who profess absolute and objective truths. Moreover, the simple fact that one says everything is relative, is in reality self-refuting because one is already stating an absolute truth that cannot be true in the first place because there is no absolute truth, as they believe. Indeed, how can one say everything is relative without implying that this is the absolute truth that he or she is trying to deny?

If one pushes this logic to the extreme, and goes with the principle that all things are relative, one then cannot find any common ground between individuals that is absolutely true. This means that chaos in society will take over and no order is possible except when it is imposed by force. But isn't this the very definition of tyranny?

Joseph Cardinal Ratzinger, who became Pope Benedict XVI, thinks it is so. In his brilliant speech of April 18, 2005, he said:

> How many winds of doctrine have we known in recent decades, how many ideological currents, how many ways of thinking. The small boat of the thought of many Christians has often been tossed about by these waves - flung from one extreme to another: from Marxism to liberalism, even to libertinism; from collectivism to radical individualism; from atheism to a vague religious mysticism; from agnosticism to syncretism and so forth. Every day new sects spring up, and what St Paul says about human deception and the trickery that strives to entice people into error (cf. Eph 4: 14) comes true.... We are building a dictatorship of relativism that does not recognize anything as definitive and whose ultimate goal consists solely of one's own ego and desires.

Modern society rejects, with accusation of dogmatism, any decision based on something that goes beyond the things that can be seen with a materialistic eye that is disguised as "scientific paradigm." Such a view is simply an attempt to ban any metaphysical reference. In his address of August 15, 2014, Pope Francis observed:

> We see signs of an idolatry of wealth, power and pleasure which come at a high cost to human lives. Closer to home, so many of our own friends and contemporaries, even in the midst of immense material prosperity, are suffering from spiritual poverty, loneliness and quiet despair. God seems to be removed from the picture. It is almost as though a spiritual desert is beginning to spread throughout our world. It affects the young too, robbing them of hope and even, in all too many cases, of life itself.

Indeed, an unstoppable flow of stimuli and information provided by a technological opulence is radically changing our collective identity marked by an obvious spiritual poverty.

The new Prometheus spirit is failing to control his products and seems to be convinced that it is capable, without any external help, to reduce the world to an easy instrument of its absolute power. Romano Guardini described it well when he said:

> Technological minds see nature as an insensate order, as a cold body of facts, as a mere given, as an object of utility, as raw material to be hammered into useful shape; it views the cosmos similarly as a mere space into which objects can be thrown with complete indifference.

This new spirit that has changed our collective identity has also changed our vocabulary. Now we talk about "low self-esteem" instead of "sin," for example. We talk about "experiencing God's affirmation" instead of "justification." We talk about "self-worth" instead of "sanctification" or even "salvation," and so on. This proves also that we are marginalizing God or, in a more subtle way, we are making God in our own image.

It is true we no longer are in the ancient world that was stuffed with multiple gods to worship. We became too sophisticated to do that. We just replaced these ancient gods with other gods. How many men and women worship their achievements, business, money, power, sex, a position, a career, or any other aspect of human life? By doing so, we determine for ourselves what is good and what is evil, we create our own values, and, more simply, we replace God by other gods.

"God is dead," said Friedrich Nietzsche. He was killed in the heart of modern men and women – killed by science and rationalism. The death of God will also end the long time accepted standards and principles of morality and of purpose, precisely because God was providing the very foundation of religious morality.

Not so fast, though. Life is not that simple. It still has its many colors.

Black/white – some things are supposed to be there, and fortunately they still are whether we admit it or not. There are still holy books. There are still traditions. There is still conscience. There is still a common ground for truth in every heart. There is still revelation. There is still inspiration. There is still discernment of the will of God that points to the right path to take. Without the living God, there could be no adequate answer to questions such as: What ought we to do? How ought we to live? Why are we here? Where are we going? What is the meaning of all this? Why is there so much violence? Why are there so many crimes and dysfunctions of all kinds?

If there is no God, how are we able to determine what to do with ourselves and with each other? What would be our destination? What would be our destiny?

"If there is no God, everything is permitted." Even if this line is not necessarily correct all the time, it nevertheless hits a nerve in our culture.

A conservative ideology would be happy to use it in scandals and crimes committed by liberals and atheists. They would say if God and his laws existed for these people, we would not have had crimes that go against God's will and his clear commandments. To such legitimate claims, a liberal mind would return the "favor" with its legitimate claims also. When conservatives become fundamentalist and perceive themselves as the chosen instruments of God's will and allow themselves to do anything – killing included – in the name of God, then "If there is God, everything is permitted" would be accurate as well.

But here is a more profound definition of God that transcends conservative and liberal minds. "God is love" (1 John 4:16). God is present when there is love between people. Then the sentence, "If there is no God, everything is permitted," is correct in the sense that when there is no love, one can commit any atrocity imaginable. However, the sentence, "If there is God, everything is permitted" is also correct in the sense that a real loving person will do only what God wants him or her to do, not to just do whatever he or she wants to do in the name of God.

Such an interpretation is not new. Saint Augustine said this about sixteen centuries ago. He said: "Love God and do as you please" (or, in another version, "Love, and do whatever you want." Here is the important and critical catch. If you really love God, you will want what he wants, what pleases him will please you, and what displeases him will necessarily displease you, and consequently you will feel like the most miserable human being on earth. In this sense, if your love for God is true, authentic, and sincere, then this love will certainly lead you to follow the highest ethical standards. Then we will be our brothers and sisters' keepers, and not killers. The radical freedom of "everything is permitted" brings with it the heavy burden of total responsibility.

Black/white – some things are still here. We know it when we realize that "God is love."

3

Modernity's Rebellion Against God

A Downing Modernity

At the time when modernity started—in the 17th century—there were no cars, no airplanes, no electricity, no Internet, no high-quality medicine, and nothing from what we enjoy using today. Most of the Western population believed that God created the world and tried to live according to defined doctrines, rules, and traditions.

But around the year 1650, something different happened: modernity. This was the era of humanity that was defined by scientific, technological, and socioeconomic changes, and characterized by an extravagant optimism and an excessive confidence in its own power to generate inevitable progress in all spheres of life. Here are some of the key points of that time in history:

a- The emphasis on the role of science and rational thought: more science and reason and less faith. People of that time started to increasingly look to science and to reason for answers to their problems and world problems at the expense of faith and superstitions of previous times. Science then was becoming the path to truth. Francis Bacon and others, for example, would gently nudge God aside and say: we do not need your help; we know now how to return to the Garden of Eden, we know how to do things by ourselves, and we know what we need to know. Putting God aside makes it impossible to turn back to religious answers for life's predicament.

b- The Enlightenment period or the "Age of Reason" of the 17th and 18th centuries: That Enlightenment, with its unambiguous insistence on the domination of intellectual, scientific, and philosophical methods for life's solutions, was a prominent illustration for new convictions. No external revelation needed. A divine revelation with its permanent body of doctrines is denied. Religion could be considered simply as a religious sentiment and an internal human experience, and doctrines and dogmas have their origin within the human consciousness.

c- Individualism: more individual freedom of thought and action. This is a shift from previous eras where individuals' lives and actions were more dictated by the social environment and political and religious institutions. Here, there is more emphasis on the personal reflection and exploration, even though social structures can still shape people and behaviors.

d- Industrialization: more labor production, more trade, and more socioeconomic status. This created two social classes: those who own factories, farms, and businesses; and those who sold effort and time to work in factories, farms, and businesses that were owned by others.

e- Urbanization: more people moving to cities for better opportunities. This meant that people had more chances for improvement and for cities more opportunities to become more developed.

f- Surging role of the state: bigger role for the state in foreign affairs and in domestic governance. This meant an increase in a centralized control of the government in everyday affairs like public education, public housing, national health, and other social issues.

g- Culture: modernism considers culture to be like science that is continuously changing and progressing. Therefore, what was proposed at one time may be overturned by the development of different situations in life.

These were some of the main characteristics of the modernity that replaced an agricultural society with an industrial one. However, we can say that, even if we seem to keep in place the main social structures that shaped the modernist society, different issues with different solutions are more prioritized in, and more suitable for, a time that can be called post-modernity. We now live in a technology/information society that is replacing little by little—or at least extending—the industrial one. Some characteristic of the new society include:

- Interconnection by using mass telecommunications networks
- Broadening social interactions and breaking down barriers in communications
- Removing time and distance between the local and the global
- Globalization of thoughts, crises, solutions, interests, threats, war and peace, terrorism, and everything we do
- Claiming of the difficulty and perhaps the impossibility the explain the new world using the old ways of thinking and traditional values of the old world
- Claiming that everyone can believe what they want to believe. Since there is no absolute truth, the answers to life's questions are always changing.
- Sex revolution, gender revolution, values revolution, and "anything" revolution
- Questioning and canceling any solid entity like God, Bible, traditions, historic figures, objective truths

- Claiming that traditions—religious, social, political, cultural—are no longer immutable deposits of faith or references to abide by, but a kind of "heritage" that can be "renewed" in the light of new experiences. This meant the death of history, the death of metaphysics, the death of objective truth, the death of God.

- Claiming that the best is the newest. and the newest is the latest

- Relativism

- Cancel culture and wokeism

- Secular Humanism: A Dream for a Society without God

- Our Human "Isms"

To summarize, one can say that modernist philosophy claims that religion is an emotion, and not objective truth, and one cannot come to know God by human reason. Modernism has been succeeded by post-modernism which can be described as an extreme form of modernism that tends to see things in more subjective, more relativistic, more skeptical, and more nihilistic ways. We can also add that, if there was certain logic during the period of modernism, the approach used in the post-modernism period is generally considered irrational and unscientific to the point of "anything goes," as it was very often said. The arrogant certainty of modernism was succeeded by the countless relative perspectives of post-modernism.

Relativism

The sentence "Truth is relative" that we hear everywhere we turn is itself relative in spite of its original intended reality that meant to be absolute and objective. If one says, "What's true for you may not be true for other people," with the intention of convincing others that this was an absolute truth, one is contradicting himself or herself since there is no absolute truth, as he or she just said. Isn't that contradictory to say there are absolutely no absolutes! So what? Contradictory or not, irrational or not, who cares provided one satisfies one's own ego and desires. At the present time, we seem to need a personal possessive pronoun in our ordinary language. We replaced "the truth," with "my truth," "your truth," "their truths." There is no objective truth. There is only subjective truth because reality is a "mental construct" and all truth is dependent on one's perspective.

In any case, we have to admit that relativism is so deeply engrained in the mindset and lifestyles of modern men and women that one frequently hears in regular conversations that "each person should decide for himself or herself what is right and what is wrong, and what is good and what is evil."

So, how to define relativism? Cambridge Dictionary says that this is "the belief that truth and right and wrong can only be judged in relation to other things and that nothing can be true or right in all situations." Stanford Encyclopedia of Philosophy says: "Relativism, roughly put, is the view that truth and falsity, right and wrong, standards of reasoning, and procedures of justification are products of differing conventions and frameworks of assessment and that their authority is confined to the context giving rise to them." Britannica Dictionary says that relativism is "the belief that different things are true, right, etc., for different people or at different times." The Free Dictionary says that relativism is "The theory that value judgments, as of truth, beauty, or morality, have no universal validity but are valid only for the persons or groups holding them." Practically, these definitions lead to the following conclusion: what is true or false for you is true or false for you, and not for me, and we should restrain ourselves from telling others that they are wrong because there is no right and wrong. Truth requires a "North Star" for guidance and criteria for verification and falsification. If there are no "North Star" and no criteria, one would enter the confusing post-truth approach.

Relativism can infiltrate our total being; it is pervasive in our culture today. We can have, for example, ethical/moral relativism that wants to submit all morals to the social group within which they are practiced. We can also have cognitive relativism that believes that there is no system of truth that is more valid and legitimate than another one, there is no objective standard of truth, and consequently there is no God of absolute truth. Also we can have what is called situational relativism that means that right and wrong are dependent upon the situation and the circumstances in which we find ourselves. Relativism can extend to any area of life that includes all religious convictions and traditions, all art forms, all political systems, all life decisions and lifestyles, etc. This means that principles are based on culture and individual choice for there are no objective rules governing right and wrong. Therefore, since there is no such thing as objective, historic, real truth, individuals and groups can spin any story according to their own interests, and no one is allowed to judge others—who am I to judge you and who are you to judge me? And, in case of severe disagreements and conflicts, just find a court willing to support your "right." Moreover, and in the sphere of religion, and because all religions are good, if a religion makes a genuine truth-claim at the expense of another religion, that religion is called "intolerant."

Although relativism may be one of the most destructive currents of our times, there is another side to it that should be considered as well. Relativists would argue that there is no possible "one size" that fits all the billions of people on earth. Also, they argue that it is undeniable that society's values change over time; slavery is no longer acceptable, for example. Other examples would be the concept of polygamy and its evolution through the centuries, and the evolving question of same-sex marriage. What worldly and human things are permanent for ever anyway? No wonder the relativists' eagerness to replace the old virtues with new ones such as pluralism, diversity, otherness, dissimilarity, distinctiveness, heterogeneousness, differentiability, and the like.

Do "Wokeness" and "Cancel Culture" Cancel God?

Once upon a time, people used principles taken from holy books to accordingly live their lives. They used to refer to the sages and the saints as living examples of what they are supposed to think about right and wrong.

Once upon a time, people used to gather on a given territory, agree on certain rules and regulations, and write a constitution that citizens of that country abide by.

Once upon a time, different groups from different parties and persuasions used to respect each other, listen to each other, and accommodate each other.

Once upon a time, there used to be some kind of collective and universal wisdom to abide by. No more. The personal experience took over and defined the terms of shaping reality and truth. Furthermore, pushing this new understanding to the extreme, some people wanted to decide for themselves if, for example, they were men, women, or no gender.

This is how it used to be until the day certain groups of people decided to abolish references, traditions, and outdated regulations and rules. How to do that? Activists, through the media, governments, corporations, institutions, colleges, demonstrations, would fiercely move ahead on attacking directly religion and family. By doing so, they are hoping to destroy all the virtues and values that keep societies bonded, morally sound, healthy, and happy. The days of what we used to call virtues and values are over. Today, and especially in the Western culture, traditional morals, ethics and values are belittled, mocked, and attacked, and references to God are obliterated. We seem very close, if we are not already there, to the point where only one set of beliefs is allowed by those in control, and other points of views are silenced and banned.

Welcome to cancel culture.

In culture cancel, power—not truth—is the way for changing things. Power dictates truth. No wonder why truth keeps changing. Power demands, and truth follows. "Do whatever I tell you, or else." Negotiations are meaningless. Only submission makes sense. Power is the fundamental force of social change.

Although cancel culture popped on the scene in the most recent years, the idea of it goes back far in time when there were two truths: your truth and my truth. It will be to your advantage to agree with my truth, and if you don't, you run the risk of being canceled. Aren't wars throughout history an illustration of such an attitude?

On a daily basis and instead of going to war every time we disagree with someone, we do use other forms of cancel culture. We can cancel a person, celebrities, groups of people, social media, and anyone who does not agree with us as a "well-deserved" punishment for their wrong opinions because our opinions are the right ones. Tell me about biases! However, in many occasions, it is not a question of biases only; it is an agenda, a message, a mission to accomplish. We do this either violently sometimes or non-violently most of the time. Here, the computer is always ready to help in targeting any person, any company, any institution, or any leader, from our comfortable room. Cancel culture activists would use ridicules, attempts to have their bank accounts removed, getting people fired, boycotting companies, stores, and any manipulating means of attempting to control others.

Such a climate of wokeness and cancel culture has its consequences in society. A lack of shared truth would cause erosion of trust and society becomes divided and fragmented. Also, the fact that individuals who have their own truth only would lead to an uncertain and confused future because of the loss of standard of what is right and what is wrong.

God, in this context, is not safe either.

God, the creator and the ultimate authority of all things, can be canceled. When people try to cancel a person, a group, an institution on the grounds of their biased religious beliefs and fanaticism, they are, in practice, canceling the supreme authority and replacing it with their own authority. In order to successfully reach the so-called "mission accomplished" goal, God must be canceled. With God canceled, civilization, as we know it, is canceled too. Such a path of darkness and confusion will lead inevitably to the law of the jungle.

Secular Humanism: A Dream for a Society without God

Is humanism for or against God?

The concept of humanism, as is the case for many other concepts like peace and love, for example, remains somewhat vague and ambiguous. The understanding of such words depends on how one wants to see things.

The philosophy of humanism brought an important contribution to the understanding of the human condition, but not in a way that was univocal and uniform. Humanism appeared under several faces and colors. Here are some of them:

Cultural Humanism. Originated mainly in Greece and Rome, and then evolved throughout Europe, cultural humanism is the rational humanism that became over time a basic part of the Western view with regard to science, ethics, law, political theory, and sometimes our understanding of religion.

Literary Humanism. This is the kind of humanism that is interested mainly in literary culture and humanities.

Renaissance Humanism. Developed especially at the end of the middle ages, this humanism wanted above all to recognize the ability of human beings to determine for themselves what is good and what is evil as well as what is true and what is false. Here, it is the human being who is the measure of all things.

Religious Humanism. Religious humanists usually insist on the functional side of religion. Religion, here, is what serves best the needs of individuals and community. It is therefore the basis for moral values, inspiring ideals, and ways for dealing with life's realities.

Educational Humanism. This humanism believes that the studies that develop the human intellect are the studies that make humans more human.

Modern Humanism. This humanism may be under other names too, such as democratic humanism, ethical humanism, scientific humanism, naturalistic humanism, and so on. This humanism rejects all that is related to supernaturalism, and relies, instead, upon reason and science.

Secular Humanism. The main roots of this humanism go back to the eighteenth-century enlightenment rationalism and the nineteenth-century free thought. A line like "What has Jerusalem to do with Athens?" would describe well this humanism; meaning that it takes side with rational heritage symbolized by ancient Athens, rather than with faith heritage symbolized by ancient Jerusalem. Therefore, this humanism rejects all activities traditionally associated with religion.

The main idea behind secular humanism is the attempt to shift the frame of reference for any philosophical, moral, artistic, political, or scientific system from the supernatural to the natural. Therefore, the highest ideals of human existence can be achieved without regard to God, a revealed religion, a holy book, or a dogma. Even though all secular humanists do not agree on everything, nevertheless they seemed to have had a certain consensus on a certain number of points gathered in Humanist Manifesto I of 1933, Humanist Manifesto II of 1973, A Secular Humanist Declaration of 1980, and Humanist Manifesto of 2003.

Here is a summary of the secular humanist's propositions that concern our chapter:

- God is not necessary; there is no need to deny or not deny God or gods. Humanists are skeptical about the existence of supernatural beings. The material universe is the only thing that exists; it is self-existent and not created by God.

- If God has nothing to do with the creation and has no role to play in daily lives, faith in God becomes irrelevant and outmoded. Consequently, any worship or prayer to God is rejected. People should then use this time in promoting social well-being. Religion may rather retard human progress.

- No need for God or for religion in order to live a happy, significant, and meaningful life. Some secular humanists go even farther by arguing that religions can sometimes constitute an obstacle for living a meaningful life because they force individuals to promote false beliefs and, accordingly, live a wasted life.

- Secular humanists believe that this is the only life we have and there is nothing beyond this life: no heaven or hell, and no reincarnation either.

- Human beings are totally physical and they evolve by natural means. Since they do not have a soul, the ultimate end of their human life is to be found in the here and now.

- Science and reason are the reliable tools for knowledge. There are no limits for their power, and no beliefs should be placed beyond their scrutiny because they are the only source of knowing the truth.

- Ethical and fulfilling lives are very important for a humanistic society. Moral values do not require the existence of God, or references to a holy book, or approval of a religious authority. The knowledge of right and wrong is shaped by science and reason as well as by the understanding of the human condition and how human beings can flourish. Thus, lessons from history and personal experience contribute greatly to the humanist moral code.

- Secular humanists put emphasis on individual moral autonomy and responsibility. They encourage the development of the intellectual and emotional skills in order to exercise this responsibility properly, and at the same time they discourage the passive, uncritical acceptance of a particular moral and religious set of rules.

- Humanists defend a secularist movement: they favor an open society and want the State to be neutral in regard to religion. The State should protect the freedom of the individuals whether they are religious or not.

- Since God and all that is related to God are not in the picture, human beings alone are responsible for the realization of the world of their dreams. They will find their way for reconciliation by solving the problems of competing political or economic systems and by overcoming their destructive ideological differences.

Some key quotations that probably most secular humanists seemed to have agreed on and cherished are very revealing. They help us understand not only their choice in regard to God but also the consequence of such a choice. Here are a few of these quotations:

Religious humanists regard the universe as self-existing and not created. (Manifesto 1)

Humanism believes that man is a part of nature and that he has emerged as the result of a continuous process. (Manifesto 1)

Religious humanism considers the complete realization of human personality to be the end of man's life and seeks its development and fulfillment in the here and now. (Manifesto 1)

Man is at last becoming aware that he alone is responsible for the realization of the world of his dreams, that he has within himself the power for its achievement. (Manifesto 1).

As nontheists, we begin with humans not God, nature not deity. (Manifesto II)

Promises of immortal salvation or fear of eternal damnation are both illusory and harmful... Modern science discredits such historic concepts as the "ghost in the machine" and "separable soul." Rather, science affirms that the human species is an emergence from natural evolutionary forces... There is no credible evidence that life survives the death of the body. (Manifesto II)

We affirm that moral values derive their source from human experience. Ethics is *autonomous* and *situational*, needing no theological or ideological sanction. Ethics stems from human need and interest. (Manifesto II)

We believe in maximum individual autonomy consonant with social responsibility" (Manifesto II)

The right to birth control, abortion, and divorce should be recognized... The many variety of sexual exploration should not be in themselves be considered 'evil.'... Short of harming others or compelling them to do likewise, individuals should be permitted to express their sexual proclivities and pursue their life-styles as they desire. (Manifesto II)

[W]e support a just distribution of nature's resources and the fruits of human effort so that as many as possible can enjoy a good life. (Manifesto III)

The responsibility for our lives and the kind of world in which we live is ours and ours alone" (Manifesto III)

We oppose any tyranny over the mind of man, any efforts by ecclesiastical, political, ideological, or social institutions to shackle free thought. (A Secular Humanist Declaration)

Compulsory religious oaths and prayers in public institutions (political or educational) are also a violation of the separation principle [of Church and State]. (A Secular Humanist Declaration)

Secular humanist ethics maintains that it is possible for human beings to lead meaningful and wholesome lives for themselves and in service to their fellow human beings without the need of religious commandments or the benefit of clergy. (A Secular Humanist Declaration)

[W]e find that traditional views of the existence of God either are meaningless, have not yet been demonstrated to be true, or are tyrannically exploitative. Secular humanists may be agnostics, atheists, rationalists, or skeptics, but they find insufficient evidence for the claim that some divine purpose exists for the universe. (A Secular Humanist Declaration)

We reject the divinity of Jesus, the divine mission of Moses, Mohammed, and other latter day prophets and saints of the various sects and denominations. We do not accept as true the literal interpretation of the Old and New Testaments, the Koran, or other allegedly sacred religious documents, however important they may be as literature. Religions are pervasive sociological phenomena, and religious myths have long persisted in human history. (A Secular Humanist Declaration)

Secular humanism places trust in human intelligence rather than in divine guidance. Skeptical of theories of redemption, damnation, and reincarnation, secular humanists attempt to approach the human situation in realistic terms: human beings are responsible for their own destinies. We believe that it is possible to bring about a more humane world, one based upon the methods of reason and the principles of tolerance, compromise, and the negotiations of difference. (A Secular Humanist Declaration)

This was the dream. Some aspects of this dream are very good and appealing to what is human in us. Indeed, who does not want happiness and fulfillment? What is wrong with willing to be the best one can be? Who does not wish for a world that is more humane with a society that knows how to solve problems, negotiate differences, and live in peace?

This dream was only a dream and remains a dream. It was just another utopia. One of James Hitchcock's conclusions that describe well this reality is the following:

The ultimate failure of Secular Humanism is in the fact that of its very nature it promises what it cannot fulfill. By encouraging people to put their trust in earthly happiness it programs them for disillusionment. This is in large measure the reason why the history of the modern world has been characterized, intellectually, by philosophies of pessimism like Existentialism and by often-rancorous bitterness over various plans for worldly improvement. In the twentieth century, mass slaughter has been perpetrated not by religious believers in opposition to heresy but by secularists convinced that their plan for a worldly utopia is the only possible one. (James Hitchcock, *What Is Secular Humanism? Why Humanism Became Secular and How It Is Changing Our World*, Ann Arbor, Michigan: Servant Books, 1982, p. 141)

In the humanist perspective, if society is founded solely on humanist ideals (false premise that there is no God, practical atheism, factual evolution, total autonomy of human beings, relative truth), unavoidable consequences are bound to occur.

With the absence of an objective and absolute truth – identified with God, as is the case in the religious mind, and opposed to the humanist mind that sees the truth as something continuously emerging and evolving – everything becomes relative. If this is the case, doesn't this include, at the same time, what secular humanists claim to be the truth also? When everything is relative and there is no point of reference for anything, every person will decide what is right and what is wrong. When every person will decide what is right and what is wrong, there will be unwillingness to follow any authority. When one is unwilling to follow authority, society won't function, and chaos will be the rule.

Then, situational ethics will flourish: everything will be justified and permitted for reasons like: "If it feels good do it," "You are OK, I am OK," "Everybody does it," "Eat, drink, and be merry for tomorrow we die"... lifestyle. Let us remember here the statement widely attributed to Dostoyevsky, "If there is no God, everything is permitted."

Then, a person becomes the measure of everything. One becomes self-righteous and practically answers only to himself or herself. He or she becomes the ultimate decider including the decision of suicide or murder because he or she makes the rules. When one makes his or her own rules, he or she can change the rules tomorrow too. What society can survive if everyone has his or her own rules?

Moreover, when there is neither a soul nor anything beyond this life, materialism becomes the philosophy of life. With materialism, thrives "utilitarianism" – the use of a spouse, a child, a friend, or any other person as a commodity. When they are no longer useful, one can just reject them and replace them with someone or something else. If bonding is bonding today, but not necessarily tomorrow, then bye-bye society! Can a society survive with the fantasy du jour?

Furthermore, the secular humanist philosophy – or "religion," we can even say – has a molten calf out of self. It teaches people to seek answers from their own feelings and minds rather than from God. It also wants them to elevate their own self-esteem by any means. No wonder one becomes so selfish, self-serving, self-indulgent, self-centered, and self-sufficient. The self can become the idol per excellence.

The simple factual truth is that, when we remove God, the Commandments, prayer, and all that is related to the divine and the sacred from our minds and daily lives, we won't replace them with the good character and the virtue – that's a mere pretension – we replace them with perversions and violence. No wonder our society finds it difficult to punish criminals; it denies the sin and the criminality of the perversion in the first place.

The idol of the self is never satisfied. The pursuits of pleasure for pleasure, money for money, comfort for comfort, power for power, and more and more, are temporary diversions of life that always give way to a deep despair. History has proved, time and again, that nothing can satisfy the self except the Infinite. This is exactly what secular humanists seek to avoid talking about. Needless to say that some of them are so optimistic that they believe that only reason and science have the power to overcome the forces of unreason, evil, and the unknown.

Pretending that, one day, we will know all the mystery of the universe by ourselves, and by ourselves alone, is utopianism.

Our Human "Isms"

Our mind wants to understand everything, and that includes what it cannot understand – God.

God is understood by faith, and faith is beyond what is rational; it is a grace.

Throughout the centuries, the mind kept trying to understand and explain the known, the unknown, and the unknowable. We seem to continue in the same way again and again, believing that the "isms" we have created may provide us with the right answer. They did not. They do not.

Let us browse through some of the "isms" that we thought might have the solution we were eagerly looking for, but we either found a dissatisfying answer or we found no answer at all.

Agnosticism. If theists profess confidence in their views with regard to the existence of God, and if atheists want to prove absolutely the non existence of God, agnostics throughout the centuries held the middle ground of not knowing whether or not God existed. For them, evidence for God's existence is balanced by evidence against God's existence. Because of the limitations of the human intellect, they prefer not to form a final judgment as to whether or not God exists.

Atheism. Atheism, generally speaking, is the absence of belief in God's existence. Some atheists find themselves practically in the categories of skepticism, indifference, or just ignorance. However, some others went further. For these, it is not a question of belief only; it is a question of hope that there is no God because they don't want to deal even with the idea that maybe there is a God. C.S. Lewis, among many others, noted the irony of the atheists' position by saying that "atheists express their rage against God although in their view He does not exist."

Deism. Deism believes in God but as a religious practice based on reason only. It does not accept supernatural revelations of any sorts. God does not intervene in the universe; God leaves the universe to run by its own laws. This is a religion without revelation that exemplifies the vast confidence in reason. Deists believe that the study of Nature and the use of reason are more helpful in understanding God than any scriptures, creeds, or traditions. Rousseau and Voltaire in France and Benjamin Franklin and Thomas Jefferson in the USA are among those who professed such beliefs.

Fundamentalism. Applied to religions, fundamentalism would be the belief that the absolute and infallible truth is found only in the inviolable "word" of God that is read literally in every word of a holy book and practiced in a sacred tradition. Such a belief has the capacity to affect deeply – and it does – the very structure of society and to become the dominant and conclusive factor in political systems.

Existentialism. Existentialism insists on being, and being cannot be the subject of an objective enquiry. Therefore, existence should be understood through a personal experience of feeling, thinking, suffering... with the will to make our own choices. If, for Kierkegaard, who is usually considered the originator of existentialism, God gives a meaning to life, for Sartre, who took Nietzsche's "God is dead" message to heart, the only resource is our freedom to choose the way we want to see the world and live in the world.

Fideism. For fideism, the essential religious doctrines cannot be established and proved by rational means. They must be accepted by faith. Faith is the only valid authority because religious experience is beyond the limits of reason and human comprehension. The finite mind cannot grasp the infinite and the unimaginable. The non-believers have used the principle of "faith alone" as a "good" reason to justify their doubts.

Jihadism. Jihadism is often defined as "holy war," but not all jihads involve combats. Personal jihad suggests the effort to be righteous and to purge one's soul of sin and worldly desires. Jihad refers also to both defensive and offensive warfare against the enemies of Islam, the infidels, and those who practice a religion that is moderate, tolerant, and secularized. At the present time, and because of some extremist groups, jihad tends to mean – wrongly – terrorism. In fact, authentic Islam with the Sharia (Muslim law) forbids the slaughter of women, children, and noncombatants.

Manichaeism. Manichaeism was an influential religious movement founded and spread by Mani, the Persian prophet. It taught a radical dualism of good and evil, light and darkness, God and matter. For the Manichaeans, the way to return to the divine source is through severe asceticism. Before his conversion to Christianity, St. Augustine was an adherent of this movement.

Materialism. Materialism is the theory that says that whatever exists is matter or is dependent on matter. Therefore, notions such as "mind," "spirit," and "God" should be rejected. But what is matter?

Philosophically speaking, materialism was ill defined; it became like a certain policy or a way of seeing the world rather than a "real" reality. We still need a clear definition of what materialism is.

Modernism. Modernism believes in the ability of the mind to attain truth. It does so through reason, reflection, observation, scientific methods, discovery, and technological advances. Many modernists assume that human dignity, morality, freedom, and progress could be preserved and fostered by reason and the human potential without reference to God. Reason, not God, is the starting point for understanding and living.

Monism. For monism, everything is reducible to a single substance because of the basic oneness of being – one essence, principle or energy. In fact, all the differences between beings are not real but illusion. Monism is closely associated with pantheism that believes that God is either, or indwells, everything. Basically there is no difference between Creator and creation. God is the "life-principle" and "all is one."

Monotheism. Monotheism is the belief that there is but one God. This God is usually given the attributes of omnipotence, omnipresence, and omniscience. This God, who is the source of morality and redemption, is intimately involved with our spiritual and physical worlds. Judaism, Christianity, and Islam are monotheistic.

Naturalism. Naturalism claims that the universe is self-existent and self-explanatory, and it operates according to natural laws. No need for any explanation that goes beyond the physical phenomena and the observable. Therefore, it rejects religion, mysticism, magic, platonic forms, and supernatural beings. It was attributed to Emile Zola for saying, "Civilization will not attain to its perfection until the last stone from the last church falls on the last priest."

Nihilism. For nihilism, there is no point or meaning for life or the universe. Therefore, all forms of morality are false and impossible, all values are baseless, and God is dead in the first place. Nothing can be really known with absolute certainty. Nothing can be communicated successfully. It is the reign of radical skepticism, absurdity, and anarchy.

Pantheism. Pantheism is the doctrine that teaches that everything is God and God is everything. This is the "All-god-ism" belief, one can say. Human beings, nature, and everything that exists constitute modes or elements of God's being. Every element of the universe is divine, and the divine is equally present in everything. God is not a distinct being in the sense of classical theism. The philosophy of Spinoza, in the West, is regarded as the classic example of this doctrine; Spinoza's God is not personal and not separate from the universe. The infinite substance is God and all things are "in" God.

Polytheism. Polytheism is the belief in the existence of many gods as opposed to monotheism that believes in the existence of one God. These gods are usually associated with different aspects of nature such as the sea, the earth, the fire, the wind, the storms, etc. Other gods are associated with other aspects of life such as fertility, motherhood, death, and rites of passage.

Postmodernism. Postmodernism excludes not only God, but also rationality as a foundation for making sense of reality and human experience. In fact, there is no universal truth, there is no universal morality, and there is no universal certainty of anything. Postmodernism is skeptical (or suspicious of) big systems and critical of views that claim to be rational, unbiased, or neutral. It rather believes that our ideas and judgments are always formed within a historical-cultural context. There are no absolute truths, no absolute values, and no absolute religious or ethical laws. There is no objectivity in anything. There is only subjectivity.

Rationalism. For rationalism, everything is explicable by "reason alone" – the world is organized in such a way that truths can be deduced by pure reason, and what we learn rationally is the real world. Therefore, religious beliefs are not taken seriously because they are irrational. Other sources of knowledge such as faith, custom, superstition and the like, are rejected. Some rationalists think that God enables human being to know the truth and the existence of God by means of reason, but most rationalists are atheist or agnostic. Rationalism wants and encourages people to think for themselves.

Relativism. Relativism sees that all truths are subjective. It maintains that ideas are the product of language, history, and cultural conventions. Therefore, they are denied any objective and universal standards. Furthermore, relativists see in relativism a sign of maturity; the "immature" society and religion rely on inviolable creeds and dogmas to insure stability, but the "mature" society and relativism know how to accept responsibility for the differences of opinion and action. Here, it seems necessary and adequate to quote what Cardinal Ratzinger (who became Pope Benedict XVI) famously said in his homily of April 18, 2005. Contrasting a steadfast faith in Christ and Church with a pernicious pluralism, he said:

How many winds of doctrine have we known in recent decades, how many ideological currents, how many ways of thinking. The small boat of the thought of many Christians has often been tossed about by these waves - flung from one extreme to another: from Marxism to liberalism, even to libertinism; from collectivism to radical individualism; from atheism to a vague religious mysticism; from agnosticism to syncretism and so forth. Every day new sects spring up, and what St. Paul says about human deception and the trickery that strives to entice people into error (cf. Eph 4: 14) comes true.

Today, having a clear faith based on the Creed of the Church is often labeled as fundamentalism. Whereas relativism, that is, letting oneself be "tossed here and there, carried about by every wind of doctrine", seems the only attitude that can cope with modern times. We are building a dictatorship of relativism that does not recognize anything as definitive and whose ultimate goal consists solely of one's own ego and desires.

We, however, have a different goal: the Son of God, the true man. He is the measure of true humanism. An "adult" faith is not a faith that follows the trends of fashion and the latest novelty; a mature adult faith is deeply rooted in friendship with Christ. It is this friendship that opens us up to all that is good and gives us a criterion by which to distinguish the true from the false, and deceit from truth. *(Cappella Papale – Mass "Pro Eligendo Romano Pontifice" – Homily of His Eminence Card. Joseph Ratzinger, Dean of the College of Cardinals, Vatican Basilica - Monday 18 April 2005)*

Secularism. Secularism denies any control or influence of religious beliefs on modern societies. Therefore, religious perceptions, values and terms of reference, can no longer run a life that should be based on the development of scientific and cultural ideas. Even though it is not necessarily anti-religious, secularism means in practice among other things: the end of religious teaching in State-funded education, the repeal of the laws that were designed to protect religiously defined values, the exclusion of religious criteria in appointments for public offices or in the application of civil rights, the denial—maybe not in theory, but certainly in practice—of the right of religious liberty, etc.

Theism. Theism believes in God rather than in a god. This God is the creator of the universe. God sustains the universe and intervenes within it in natural and non- natural ways. God is the primary cause of all that was, is, and will be. God is personal, omnipotent, omniscient, and omnipresent in the creation but distinct from it. Judaism, Christianity, and Islam can be considered the three major theistic religions.

Transhumanism. Wikipedia explains:

Transhumanism (abbreviated as H+ or h+) is an international cultural and intellectual movement with an eventual goal of fundamentally transforming the human condition by developing and making widely available technologies to greatly enhance human intellectual, physical, and psychological capacities. Transhumanist thinkers study the potential benefits and dangers of emerging technologies that could overcome fundamental human limitations, as well as the ethics of developing and using such technologies. The most common thesis put forward is that human beings may eventually be able to transform themselves into beings with such greatly expanded abilities as to merit the label *posthuman.*

This means that we can now control our own evolution and fundamentally transform our human condition. Indeed, our developing technologies will help us to greatly enhance our physical, intellectual, and psychological capacities. This evolution will lengthen human life and enable everyone to enjoy better minds and bodies. Moreover, this means that, by trying to play the Creator, we are trying to control everything including our human nature, and we do this by taking God's place. This way, when "God does not exist" or when "God is dead," we won't have a definition for our human nature, as Jean-Paul Sartre claimed. He said that "There is no human nature, since there is no god to conceive it." Consequently, it will be up to us to define our human nature as we want, and to choose our own life purposes as we wish. Such a liberty, without a definition of human nature, one must conclude, is founded on an atheistic ground.

All these "isms" that are mentioned here—many other "isms" could have been mentioned also—lead to the conclusion that humans are trying by any means to make themselves God. The reality is that the way God is conceived, so is conceived our outlook on life. The "religious" outlook is at the core of our culture, politics, economics, values, and the way we think, act, and live.

Part Two

Bricks and Mortar of the Modern Tower

4

Bricks and Mortar of the Modern Tower (1)

Auguste Comte (1798 - 1857)

Auguste Comte (1798-1857) was a French positivist philosopher. He was known for his theory of positivism and for being one of the founding fathers of sociology (the word "sociology" is generally considered as coined by him). Also, he can be regarded as one of the philosophers, if not the first philosopher and social theorist, of science in the modern sense of the word. He believed that a scientific society was incompatible with God and that they could not co-exist together. However, since God and religion, as he understood it, have separate entities, he saw that religion could survive the "death" of God for the sake of humanity— religion seeks to understand, love, and serve humankind. Essentially, social sciences and natural sciences should be studied in the same way. In this spirit, and within his positivism philosophy, Comte claimed that human societies developed historically in three stages (the law of three stages):

1. The theological stage. This is the stage in which phenomena are explained through the use of "God," divine beings, and

supernatural entities such as ghosts, spirits, demons, etc., miraculous powers, and magic. This stage was generally seen as the stage of the civilizations of the distant past that counted on fetishism, polytheism, and monotheism to answer their questions.

2. The metaphysical stage. This is the stage in which phenomena are explained by abstractions and notions such as essences and final causes. People believed in the abstract forces rather than the supernatural to have answers for their questions.

3. The positive stage. This is the stage in which phenomena are explained by rigorous scientific methods. The task of the sciences is to study the facts and regularities of nature and society, and formulates laws. Humankind reached full maturity at this stage after leaving behind the pseudo-explanations of the theological and metaphysical phases. For Comte, the word "Positive" carries the meaning of what is scientifically certain or assured, and not as opposed to "negative." People rely on science, rational thought, and empirical laws to answer their questions. This, according to Comte, will fix our problems and allow progression and peace in societies. Author Vincent P. Miceli observed: "The positivism of Comte was aimed at shocking atheists forward into becoming anti-theists. The battle cry of their regime of science would be: 'Nothing is absolute, everything is relative!' With God and his metaphysician mourners driven forever from the human predicament, a new spiritual power would be free to unify mankind in universal maturity."

The "death" of God occurs, according to Comte, during the positive stage. But this does not necessarily mean death of religion. As a sociologist, Comte thinks that a true socialist must study society not only to understand it, but also to find better solutions for a better society. He thinks that human behavior must obey particular laws and that, if we discover these laws, we could eliminate moral evils in the same way medical scientists eliminate much of the physical suffering. Here comes the new religion he proposed—the religion of humanity. Just as the previous religions, this new one has its own pillars, sacraments, hymns, songs, prayers, calendar, feasts, and holidays. Worshiping God is replaced by honoring the great men in history, and the new god is no other than the human race—Humanity. Such worship would inspire the individual to love and make sacrifices for the benefits of humankind. Therefore, there is no personal God in the system. Instead, there is Humanity, "the great being" that is the object of veneration and cult. Could we perhaps say that some of the global elite of our days, who practice the cult of humanity by reducing individuals to social functionaries, are practicing the cult of the abstract humanity at the expense of the concrete individual here and now? Or could Comte be considered one of the fathers of the modern functionalism and utilitarianism?

Charles Darwin (1809-1882)

Charles Darwin (1809-1882) was an English scientist who was known for his doctrines of organic evolution. But what was his theory about God? Did he believe in God or not? Was he religious or not? Was he really genuine in his ideas about religion and ethics or not?

The reader of philosophy and science would have a hard time to determine clearly where Darwin really stands vis-à-vis such questions and this for several reasons. First, Darwin appeared to have evolved over the years; second, he did not want to upset his wife who was devout; third, he did not want to embarrass and upset religious people and public opinion since he needed them to advance his theory of evolution; and fourth, he might have been lacking some genuineness and ingenuousness. No wonder he can write for example, "In my most extreme fluctuations I have never been an atheist in the sense of denying the existence of God," and "I hardly see how religion and science can be kept...distinct, but...there is no reason why the disciples of either school should attack each other with bitterness." But he also can write, "Science has nothing to do with Christ," and "I do not believe in the Bible as a divine revelation, and therefore not in Jesus Christ as the son of God."

During his early years, he seemed to have used a religious language such as "God bless you," "God only knows," "I wish to God," and the like. He even went to Cambridge University to study to become an Anglican priest, but somehow he was worried about declaring allegiance to the dogmas of the Church of England. Also, he felt that referring to God would not be helpful when he felt that science should be objective in nature. Here are a few points to remember when trying to understand his position in regard to God:

1. Darwin seems to have believed in God and he mentioned him many times. In his evolutionary theory, God is the creator but he does not intervene in the natural processes of evolution where no place is left for the Bible and miracles. In a letter, he explicitly wrote, "I do not believe in the Bible."

2. God's Darwin was not the personal God of Christianity. His God created the world, but then he let it run without any divine involvement. God has no influence in the evolutionary development in any way. At a certain point of his life, Darwin went a step further to speculate that life may have arisen without divine intervention. Such positions would lead us to believe that he might have been a deist and perhaps an agnostic as he, himself, stated, "I for one must be content to remain an Agnostic." So he seemed to have moved from Christian belief in a personal God to a deistic approach, to end up in an agnostic position. One can perhaps say that Darwin was not an atheist in the full sense of the word, and he was not a believer in the full sense of the word also. Clearly, Darwin was not consistent in the language he

used to describe his beliefs. His kind of theism wants to see a supernatural deity at the origin of the universe but did not intervene in the course of history. But he also thinks that it would be inaccurate to suggest that the deity is unable to effect its purposes through natural causes.

3. Since he rejected the divine intervention in his evolutionary theory, it was normal for him to reject the religious basis for morality as well. For him, morality comes from natural evolutionary processes and not from God. Therefore, morality is neither universal nor unchanging. By this, he distanced himself from a Judeo-Christian conception of morality.

4. The essential idea behind the evolution theory is that the natural process has no need for the supernatural. Therefore a personal God is useless, and one has no need to believe in him. Moreover, if evolution is the right way to go, then the Bible is the false one. No harmony is possible between the theory of evolution and the creationist concept of the Bible.

5. Among other things in the Bible, Darwin rejected the doctrine of future judgment. He clearly stated: "I can indeed hardly see how anyone ought to wish Christianity to be true; for if so the plain language of the text seems to show that the men who do not believe, and this would include my Father, Brother and almost all my best friends, will be everlastingly punished. And this is a damnable doctrine."

6. Sometimes Darwin seems to believe that this wonderful universe could not be the result of chance alone. Some other times, he does not want to admit that there is a design behind the structures of living organisms. There has been a high degree of ambiguity, equivocation, and doublespeak in Darwin's references to the deity.

However, and in spite of all this, one could learn a lesson of humility for there are no simple answers for the ultimate questions of existence, and one should learn to discern the path of truth.

Karl Marx (1818-1883)

Karl Marx (1818-1883) was a German social theorist who was interested above all in economics and history. He was an atheist and secular humanist. For him, there is only the natural, material world. He believed in absolute humanism in which the human being is the Supreme Being, not God, for there is neither spiritual world nor life after death.

Marx atheism seems to be based on the following postulates:

1. Matter is the supreme and unique cause of everything. This can be called dialectical materialism. In the steps of German philosopher George W.F. Hegel, Marx thinks that in everything there is a thesis, an antithesis, and synthesis. From what things are (thesis) to their opposite (antithesis) emerges the result of the struggle (synthesis). The synthesis will in turn become a new thesis opposed to antithesis with a new synthesis. Such a constant struggle will continue to lead to more advanced levels. New ideas are created out of the old. The idea of the present will always challenge the sacred ideas of the past. For Marx, "Events are born out of the conflict of social forces and then resolved into a unity of opposites."

2. The economic structure carries all the structures of society. This can be called historical materialism. Marx used historical materialism to say that history is rather the result of material conditions than the result of ideas. In this context, he explained that social structures, laws, morality, religion, and any other things are rooted in economics in the first

place. All the institutions in our daily lives—government, church, marriage, arts, business, etc.—are dependent on the economic forces, and can be truly understood in that context. One can, then, conclude that all human behavior is determined by the economic realities and the class struggle between those who own things and those who do not own things. Marx seems obsessed by the idea of economics that runs human history. Humans' main concerns are, according to him, the material ones that lead the way before any other grand ideas. Such a materialist perspective sets forth the lived experiences of poverty, misery, exploitation, and oppression.

3. Marx tried to build a social, political, and economic system based on the struggles between capitalists and working class. The focus is to reach a reality of common ownership characterized be the absence of social classes, money, family, and state.

4. The human being is Supreme Being. This can be called absolute humanism. Here is the focal point of Marx's atheism. In his view, there is no superior being over the human being. That is why, it is important for human beings to be aware of their dignity and do all that is necessary to reach that level of superiority. In order to achieve that goal, Marx finds that it is necessary to destroy what stands in the way of achieving such a goal. He wants to destroy the family, individuality and private property, capitalism and the free market, the bourgeois society and the nation, and the past and eternal truths.

5. When Marx says "The religious world is but the reflex of the real world," he is saying that religion, like any other institution in society, depends on the productive forces. Therefore, doctrines and beliefs are irrelevant. What could be relevant, though, is what religion could offer to society—

what purpose and social action religion can serve, and not its beliefs.

6. All in all, Marx dislikes religion because he finds it irrational and hypocritical. Religion may preach valuable principles but, in reality, it sides itself with the oppressors. It provides reasons and excuses to keep society going as it is with its classes' struggle, inequality, and injustice. Its high ideals and the unknowable god it preaches help to make people more amenable to accept the status quo. It creates the illusory fantasies of finding happiness in the next life while sticking with the miseries of this life. Instead of trying to fix the underlying causes of people's suffering, religion would use the imaginary "drug" of the happy hope of the future to help the oppressors, who are responsible for the pain and suffering, maintain their position in keeping things as they are. The illusory happiness that religion creates in people makes them flee from the real world into a comforting state of mind that is an illusion. In this sense, religion creates a false interpretation of reality.

7. By rejecting God-centered religion, Marx opts for a human-centered religion. He thinks that it is up to humans to define what being human means and how to be human. Therefore, humans are the creators of reality by shaping and controlling their physical and social environments and circumstances. By doing so, they will shape themselves. They are the only reality, the only meaning of the universe, and the only force that drives evolution and history. Marx wrote: "The religion of the workers has no God because it seeks to restore the divinity of man."

8. Also, Marx's communism had the ambition to abolish all religion and all morality because they are used for social control used by the bourgeoisie to keep the proletariat satisfied and at peace with the unequal conditions of

oppression. For him, "religion is the sigh of the oppressed creature, the sentiment of heartless world, as it is the spirit of spiritless conditions. It is the opium of the people," and "the idea of God is the keynote of a perverted civilization. It must be destroyed." Marx also writes: "It is therefore, the task of history, once the other world of truth has vanished, to establish the truth of this world."

5

Bricks and Mortar of the Modern Tower (2)

Friedrich Nietzsche (1844 - 1900)

Friedrich Nietzsche (1844-1900) was a German writer and philosopher who straightforwardly announced the death of God. He famously wrote, "God is dead! God remains dead! And we have killed him!" But what does to kill God really mean? Isn't God supposed to be eternal, and thus cannot die? No, would Nietzsche say, "God" is a fiction, "God" is the product of our minds, and "God" does not exist in the first place. Here are some points that explain Nietzsche's concept of God.

1. The idea of God can be justified according to Nietzsche. It brings some solace to a world filled with senseless suffering and misery. People in hardship, distress, and despair would be willing to create a higher power who can offer help and consolation. Believing in God ensures that there will be everlasting peace and justice no matter the discomfort one goes through here. Since there is an eternal divine place, there is hope. The idea of God offers light in the middle of the darkness of the world.

2. In spite of its possible benefit, the idea of the belief in God should be dropped. Instead, we are supposed to develop our own values, define our own conditions, and achieve our own goals. We are supposed to establish our own truth. When Nietzsche says, "God is dead," he did refer to the narrow religious definition of God, but he also meant to go further and include the idea of the universal and transcendent truth. Therefore, it wouldn't be an exaggeration if we equate "God is dead" with "Truth is dead." When he speaks about God, he speaks of a broader faith "the Christian faith, which was also Plato's, that God is truth, that truth is divine." Now, "[W]e have abolished the world of truth," Nietzsche proclaimed; "nothing is true." Casting out the very ground on which certainty is based opens the door to nihilism and relativism where nothing is solid; everything becomes liquid or vaporous for, in fact, "There are no facts, only interpretations," as Nietzsche would like to say. This means, as he put it, "the whole [...] European morality," is bound to "collapse." In other words, "God is dead" refers to the death of Christianity with its doctrines and moral teachings. This is also the declaration of the replacement of the religious worldview with the profane. The religion that became a tool of social control is not acceptable.

3. Since we have identified the sociological base of religion, and we no longer have a use for God as a cultural reality, we are now on our own. Nietzsche thinks that we have discovered our own answers to life questions. The ascetic ideal that Christianity has championed goes back to the dualistic world view, according to Nietzsche, and it should be rejected. The self-denial and the acceptance of deserved suffering as a preparation for a better existence in a future life have no place in a system of the life affirming of the mighty Superman, he is eager to create. The Superman

creates and masters the values he lives by, and he won't be restrained by what society defines as right or wrong.

4. In Nietzsche's thoughts, Christianity is Plato's philosophy under the disguise of religion that he describes as "Platonism of the people." He would never accept the approach of both Plato and Christianity's approach that seems to place more emphasis on an afterlife than on day-to-day existence. He does not want to hear of a transcendent world. He does not want to recognize the God of the transcendent world who rewards believers with eternal life at the expense of a devalued human existence. If "Anything real must be understood historically," as he says, then the very question "How historically God came to existence" would undermine this very God.

5. For Nietzsche, the Christian God is responsible for creating intellectual and moral simpleton, defeated, and imbecile people. In his book, *The Antichrist*, he unambiguously wrote: "The Christian conception of God—God as god of the sick, God as a spider, God as a spirit—is one of the most corrupt conceptions of the divine ever attained on earth.... God degenerated into the *contradiction* of life, instead of being its transfiguration and eternal Yes! God as the declaration of war against life, against nature, against the will to live! God—the formula for every slander against 'the world,' for every lie about the 'beyond' God—the deification of nothingness, the will to nothingness pronounced holy!"

Sigmund Freud (1856-1939)

Sigmund Freud (1856-1939) was an Austrian physician, founder of psychoanalysis. For him, God was invented by human beings out of desire and necessity to find security in the midst of a distressing, anxious, and fearful world. Here is how he came to such a conclusion:

1. In his psychoanalytic works, Freud saw that the psyche (personality) is structured into three parts: the id, the ego, and the super-ego. The id is the primitive, instinctual, impulsive (and unconscious) part of the mind. The super-ego constitutes the moral conscience and reflects society's moral values. The ego is the rational and realistic (and conscious) part that mediates between the desires of the id and the demands, orders, and moral constraints of the super-ego. Conflicts in the unconscious between the id, ego, and super-ego, according to Freud, cause mental illness.

2. Freud thinks that religious beliefs lack rational foundation and the concept of God cannot be a realistic concept for it is wishful thinking and an illusion. Therefore, the belief in God must be considered as an "infantile neurosis"—a disorder of the mind. Freud wrote: "They [religious beliefs] are illusions, fulfillments of the oldest, strongest, and most urgent wishes of mankind. We call belief an illusion when a wish-fulfillment is a prominent factor in its motivation and in doing so we disregard its relation to reality, just as the illusion itself sets no store by verification."

3. Since human beings live in a dreadful and calamitous world, and out of fear and a desire to protect themselves from this kind of world, it would be so natural for them to invent an imaginary father figure—God—who is simply a projection of their wishes. This father figure—God—became powerful in the mind of human beings and made them religious and obedient people. Another reason for being obedient, Freud suggests, would emerge from a deep feeling of guilt as a result of the Oedipus complex (Freudian theory of the child's

unconscious hostility towards his father because of the infant's sense of unity with his mother.)

4. Even though Freud notices people's great wish for a God that exists, and to whom they can turn to in their needs, he still thinks that God's existence is simply a fantasy. But people continue to choose to believe in God anyway because this God represents a powerful father-figure. "They [the believers]," wrote Freud, "give the name of 'God' to some vague abstraction which they have created for themselves."

5. Since the super-ego is the provider of the moral standards by which the ego functions, the negative effects of religion on society are enormous. Doctrines, ideologies, interpretations, or any other expression of a religious thought that are followed blindly will greatly affect perception, suppress emotions, and cause a life of hypocrisy. Needless to say, however, that a well balanced super-ego will also effect opposite results.

6. Freud thinks that the psychoanalysis therapy's role would be to release repressed emotions and make the unconscious conscious. Thus, faith, for him, arises from the deepest needs and desires that are founded upon the most powerful instincts of human nature. In this sense, God fulfills the deepest, strongest, and most urgent needs. But such a God can also be the product of neurotic and obsessive fantasies. Here, the legitimate questions would be: Can psychoanalysis help to determine what is real and what is not?

7. Although professing atheism, Freud admits that religious faith has provided comfort for people throughout history. Also he sees that the concept of taking an invisible God into the mind may benefit the individual immeasurably by the simple fact of giving that individual the capacity for abstraction. This creates the dynamics of inner life and

prepares the ground for science, literature, law, art, and the other fields of creativity.

John Dewey (1859-1952)

John Dewey (1859-1952) was an American psychologist, educationist, and a pragmatist philosopher who rejected the supernatural and considered idealism as pragmatically useless. He emphasized the practical and experimental to scientifically evaluate any belief or statement about the world without references to supernatural forces or abstractions for a credible explanation of things. His naturalistic view led him to believe that knowledge was the result of the interaction between organism and environment, and his dream was to make philosophy as practical as possible. In such a context, what would be the place of God and religion? Here are some elements that help answering this question.

1. Embracing a scientific understanding of the world, Dewey considers that supernaturalism that emerged with ancient cultures is obsolete and no longer worth believing in. Therefore, a dogmatic religion should not have anymore the authority and reverence it once had.

2. Dewey was one of the architects of the philosophical school of pragmatism that was concerned with what works, with the focus on problem solving. His pragmatism's program was considered an attempt to revolutionize the public school system. He wanted the students to learn experientially in what is known as "progressive education." This way, God and his word are replaced with secular humanism. The education, then, is no longer concerned with passing down values and traditions, but with focusing on the child, not God. It is the experiential learning rather than passing down knowledge from teachers to students. With this, Dewey

seems to advocate the idea of considering human nature as continuously changing, and consequently, fixed values and beliefs are unfavorable to progress. In such a case, schools should not be instruments to teach traditional religious and moral values. Instead, they should be focusing on the child's impulses and whims. Teachers should no longer impose abstract and external principles on students. Instead, they should help students through hands-on activities. Truths should not be thought. Truths should rather be discovered. They are not fixed and unmoving. They rather keep changing according to changing circumstances.

3. Perhaps Dewey is not considered an atheist in the true sense of the word. At times, he was even critical of atheism. However, his understanding of God is unconventional. For him, God is not the super being with supernatural powers— an ontologically prior God who created life and the universe. Coexisting with the concept of democracy, God is reduced to human ideals and human values. In this sense, God is still useful, for without "God," humanity would feel a loss. Dewey wanted to continue using the word "God" in spite of his belief that such being did not exist. Science and democracy, and not supernatural powers, are seen as parts of "religious" experience that leads to humanity's growth and progress.

4. Even without God, it is good to keep religion in place. Religion, Dewey thinks, has its way to gather people in community and invite them to act together toward ideals. Whatever makes people want to strive to be their best, that could be their "god." Thus, any experience can be religious if it brings about a better life, and not because of its "religious' content.

5. Religious revelation has been replaced by democracy that became the kingdom of God on earth. Relying on democracy

and scientific methods, humans no longer feel the need for supernatural revelation.

6. A sense of history is important and we should learn from the grand moments of human experience. But the past cannot be seen as the storage of final truths. The past should rather be considered as the fertile ground of ideals that help to accomplish a better and greater-yet-to-come life.

7. All in all, "There is no god and there is no soul," wrote Dewey. And he continued: "Hence, there is no need for the props of traditional religion. With dogma and creed excluded, then immutable truth is dead and buried. There is no room for fixed and natural law or permanent moral absolutes."

6

Bricks and Mortar of the Modern Tower (3)

Jean-Paul Sartre (1905-1980)

Jean-Paul Sartre (1905-1980) was a French philosopher and novelist. He was the greatest existentialist of the 20th century. He rejected the existence of God mainly because he wanted the individuals to be in absolute freedom for thinking, choosing their destinies, creating themselves, behaving, and acting. Such an absolute freedom wouldn't be possible with the existence of God. Sartre built a philosophical system that can be summarized in the following points.

1. Challenging traditional philosophy, Sartre grounded his philosophy on the principle that existence comes before essence—essence being the unchanging, universal, and constant nature of things, and existence being the changing, transient, and contingent reality. This practically means that humans first exist, and then they go on building their essence through actions and experiences. People are fully responsible for their actions and circumstances. It is not true, according to Sartre, to depend on essence or nature that is

pre-established by divine or universal orders. Humans define themselves and, consequently, are nothing else but what they make of themselves. Through choices and actions, they, themselves, will define their essence—identity, character, and values and principles for these are not something they were born with. This means we are negating the existence of a preordained blueprint of our lives, and this, above all, means there is no divine power who conceived a fixed essence/nature before our birth, and there is no God with a design and purpose in mind.

2. Since there is no God, no God's will, and no God's words, principles, and values, humans must freely invent their own principles, goals, and purposes. If there is a God, then the individual cannot be free. Sartre believes that there is no God to create and design the individual for the nature of the individual comes not from God, but from the person's own choices.

3. Since nothing really exists except the phenomenon of existence itself, it would be mere chimeras to imagine the reality of some kind of transcendent and infinite higher power called God. And since God cannot exist, no absolute, universal, and fixed values, and no mandatory moral laws, can exist either.

4. The concept of absolute freedom is a paramount concept in the philosophy of Sartre. The individual has unlimited freedom, and it is not only the freedom to choose and the ability to act, but it is also the freedom that shapes consciousness and essence. This means that we are responsible not only for our actions but for our circumstances as well. Therefore, we cannot blame external factors for our unhappiness, for example. Instead, we should acknowledge our role in taking the path of shaping our

destiny, rejecting the idea of being just passive recipients of external stimuli and incentives.

5. This kind of human nature understanding has the potential of allowing the change and growth we desire. Sartre is adamant in reminding us that no traditional beliefs and norms—religious, social, political, or otherwise—should play any role in our self-definition. Absolute freedom that has no limitation will define our essence, and never predefined structures. Individuals will discover their own unique purpose and shape their own existence. They will create an essence for themselves, and a structure for the world. Such an absolute freedom is irreconcilable with the existence of God. For if God exists and is the creator of what determines what it means to be human, then there is no freedom. Instead, there would be determinism.

6. Sartre draws a distinction between what he calls the *"en-soi"* (in-itself) and the *"pour-soi"* (for-itself). The *"en-soi"* applies to things, and the *"pour-soi"* applies to humans. A thing exists in itself and had definite structure—it is what it is. The individual is a *"pour-soi,"* not *"en-soi."* The individual is a project. Humans project themselves to distant goals and values, and they define their own nature. They want to be something they are not. They are *"pour-soi,"* not *"en-soi."* Now, if the *"pour-soi,"* which is the conscious self that does not have a stable identity and is always on the move, tries to define itself according to social expectations and labels others put on it, then the *"pour-soi"* tends to lie to itself. Sartre calls this *"mauvaise foi"* (bad faith) because people would deceive themselves thinking that they cannot make choices for fear of the possible consequences that choices would bring. They pretend they don't have the freedom to make choices. The truth is that individuals, according to him, are responsible for creating their own

meaning and purpose through choices and actions, because life itself has no inherent purpose and meaning.

7. Authenticity is a central theme in Sartre's philosophical system and was offered as a fundamental value. The authentic individuals know that they are radically free, completely responsible for this freedom, and that this very freedom is shaping their own beings. Sartre believes in the rejection of traditional religions and societies' established norms, and calls for the authenticity in one's existence. Unlike other philosophers who based their approaches to life on objective reason, Sartre based his vision on the human experience and the way humans define their beings through their own decisions and actions.

Where do Sartre's philosophy and his conviction of the non-existence of God lead? Author Vincent P. Miceli wrote: "… [I]n the last analysis Sartre's philosophy leads logically and directly to despair and suicide…. His world of atheism is a kingdom of nothingness plunged into intellectual darkness, convulsed with spiritual hate and peopled by inhabitants who curse God and destroy each other in their vain attempt to seize His vacant throne."

Albert Camus (1913-1960)

Albert Camus (1913-1960) was a French writer and philosopher. The question, "What is the meaning of life?" that was one of the most fundamental philosophical questions throughout centuries was an obsession for Albert Camus, and he eagerly wanted to deal with it. He did it through his novels, *The Stranger, The Plague, The Fall,* and especially through his philosophical essay, *The Myth of Sisyphus* and *The Rebel.* His conclusion was that life had no meaning and nothing can be a source of meaning, and there was no larger meaning to our existence.

Therefore, it is absurd to go on with the human quest to find meaning. Consequently, he wondered whether suicide could be the logical and adequate response to the absurdity of life. Could suicide be the normal response to the absurdity of life? Camus was haunted by such a question.

But where is God in all of this? Did Camus believe in God? Here are some points to consider when answering these questions.

1. Despite his rejection of religion and an afterlife reality, Camus respected Christians and liked to have a dialogue with them because their religion may provide some comfort to many people, although it cannot provide a genuine meaning for life.

2. What was important for him is living in the present moment, and he did not care about the idea of a transcendent being. He was interested in exploring the idea of Christian love and how it would and should work in modern society, here and now. For him, religion failed to give meaning for life, but he was not hostile towards those who believed in God, and he wanted to keep the focus on those individuals who were able to help in coping with the present moment. The present moment cannot remain fixed and unaffected by history. New moments bring new problems and require new solutions. No rules based on "Eternal principles" revealed by God. The fact is that people are constantly struggling to cope with their existing historical and constantly changing conditions.

3. Camus chose freedom and was more comfortable with opting to live without God. His atheism was not developed from an intellectual and abstract framework, but from the experience of absurdity in daily life. Daily life is filled with continuous confrontations between the individual and the world. Indifference, hostility, monotony of inescapable routine, violence, war, arbitrary suffering, despotic capriciousness, injustice, and many, many more unwelcome

adversities prove that the world is irrational and that humans live in the wilderness of inhumanity. It is resentment against the absurd that pushed Camus to adopt the attitude of total unbelief. This is why one can say that his atheism stems from his dynamic concern about men and women and their society.

4. Camus' main objection to such an attitude was the failure of religion to provide an answer to the problem of evil and suffering—the needless suffering of the innocent is the worst kind of suffering. He could not understand how an omnipotent and good God would be able to permit the widespread suffering and injustice in the world. For him, a loving God and continuous violence, famine, and misery on earth are irreconcilable. God's existence would rather make life more absurd, not less. He opted to leave God alone—if he exists, he does nothing—and counted on the individuals to create their own meaning and values in life. People, he thought, should, and are, able to work together, without counting on a transcendent being, to reduce suffering and find solutions for the problems of the present moment.

5. It is in this context that Camus saw the importance of Christianity and its positive and concrete impact on individuals and communities. Camus seems to be saying that God—if God exists—is never separated from history. Here it could be appropriate to mention that some critics of Camus described him as a "religious thinker in irreligious disguise." No wonder he continuously wrote about topics such as God, the meaning of life, sin, guilt, innocence, suffering, death, and how to live facing the future. Through the struggles of such a journey, one could feel the nuances of certain nostalgia for God.

6. So, no external source—such as religion or a higher power--exists to control one's own life, provides meaning for life,

and dictates how one should live. While embracing the absurdity of life, it is up to the individuals to responsibly determine how they should live whether God exists or not.

7. Camus concernedly examines human solidarity and the responses in the face of evil, the indifferent universe, and the absurdity of life. He thought that this is how one lives a meaningless life to the fullest without God.

Jacques Derrida (1930-2004)

Jacques Derrida (1930-2004) was a French philosopher and writer. He is widely discussed among the practitioners of "deconstruction." But is it possible to deconstruct God? Here are a few points to consider in answering the question.

1. The word "deconstruction" might be one of the latest fashionable and buzz terms in our culture today. It seems especially associated with the deconstructionist philosophical movement introduced by Jacques Derrida in the second half of the 20th century. For Derrida, the words we use have no fixed meaning. And in such a case, that would mean that people who believe in God's words of the Bible, for example, will find themselves in big troubles to follow what they believe.

2. Deconstructionism then will force believers to rely on society to define the concepts of faith, peace, justice, and God. The people in power—religious or secular—would use holy books, traditions, and doctrines to enhance their power at the expense of others who are denied the right to this same power. So, deconstruction is, then, a method that allows questioning the meanings, assumptions, inconsistencies, contradictions, motivations, biases, flaws, paradoxes, ambiguities, and values of words and concepts. Therefore,

the idea that there is a fixed or objective meaning in texts is clearly challenged—meaning is a human creation, not divine revelation or absolute truth. All depends on how individuals conceive the truth at a certain moment in time and space in their contexts of their cultural, political, religious, and environmental experiences.

3. According to Derrida, here is the thing: if something is constructed by an individual or a group, it can be de-constructed, and this applies to objects as well as to concepts. Whatever we construct, we can de-construct. Whether God exists or not, the only "God" that really counts is the one we conceive—the one culturally constructed.

4. Who and what is God? If really one wants to understand God, one should not look further than how the word 'God' is used. Somehow we seem to be convinced that a word, a concept, a text, has a fixed meaning for all times when the meaning has, in fact, all things to do with the culture, the location, and the time where a word has been used.

5. When we sometimes try to hide our troubles, cracks, messes, and confusion behind a façade of order cramming our flaws into the back of our closet, a positive deconstruction may be used to pull apart the beliefs we've carried around over the years and see what we are supposed to do with them. It is good to be able to disconnect from the junk of man-made religion and hold onto the connection with the divine.

6. Deconstruction will throw a light on the what, how, why, when, where, who, and the purpose of what has been said. If we do that, we will realize how immersed we are in our cultural biases when we thought we were living happily the objective truth. Derrida, according to some critics, seems to allow any and many interpretations for a concept, even if these interpretations are contradictory. After all, who could possibly know all things or anything about this or that

"reality"? Of course we are interested in what happens, but we should be more interested in the reason why things happen the way they happen.

7. To the question asked by St. Augustine, for example, "What do I love when I love my God?" Augustine is sure that there is a revealed answer to it, Derrida does not. When people of faith know to whom they pray, Derrida does not. The belief that one has reached the single correct meaning for "God" or "truth" could be a wonderful excuse for describing those with whom one disagrees as "heretics" or "fools" or "mentally ills," and the like. The Derrida's deconstruction may have concerns about such a strategy of exercising power in order to maintain the position of leadership among those who supposedly speak for God. Deconstruction can be good, but not when it uproots love, truth, grace, and God.

8. It is important to know that Derrida does not endorse the popular meaning of "deconstruction" that many individuals and groups are using at the present time. Indeed it would be wrong to use this word in the sense of dismantling the opinions, legitimacy, and value of others. "To deconstruct" was not meant to be a tool to subdue others by declaring their inferiority and revealing their subconscious or ill motives. Deconstruction should not be reduced to just critically questioning traditional ways of seeing the world, approaching things, and refusing to recognize the authorities in place.

Part Three

God's Substitutes

7

Our Golden Calves (1)

The Power of Modern Idols

For better or worse, our culture is forcing us to proclaim allegiance to a different set of priorities, values, and references. Consequently, our interests and goals became different now; they became our destination, if we still have a clear and recognizable one.

Upside down things seem to have been taking shape these days.

If we just watch television programs and shows, navigate the websites of the Internet, use any electronic device, or listen to what people are usually talking about, we cannot help but being struck by the enormous amount of time and effort people are devoting for their idols du jour.

Idols are everywhere – in sports, in music, in the television and movie industries, in fashion, in art, in philosophy, in religion, in war and peace, in the self... in every aspect of our lives. We may no longer worship stars, animals, statues, images, and the pagan gods, but have developed a world filled with other gods that our culture has generously provided.

We sent God back to the heavens and we settled with the gods we've created. No wonder references shifted, priorities twisted, and values took a new turn. Idols run our lives.

How to Make a God

Making a god is easy. We've done it so many times, and for so long in human history, and we are still doing it—everyday and everywhere.

Indeed, every time we let anything absorb the energy of our heart and imagination, we prove one more time that we can do it again and again because we simply prove that there is something more important than God. In fact, even if we claim to believe in God, we may be clinging to an image of God that is different from what God truly is, or we may be creating a new god altogether. This is what is called idolatry. Here Voltaire (1694-1778), the French writer, famously commented that God created us in God's image and that we have returned the compliment and created God in our own image. Indeed we have returned the compliment in a big way by transforming our world into a factory of gods at all levels—personal, social, physical, emotional, mental, and spiritual. We have, as St. Paul wrote, "exchanged the glory of the immortal God for images resembling a mortal human being or birds or four-footed animals or reptiles" (Romans 1:23).

We should never think that idolatry is something that belongs only to the past, or to pagan cultures, or to people of far lands. Idolatry is right here right now. The First Commandment was written not only for the Israelites, but for humankind of all times and places. God said, "You shall have no other gods before me. You shall not make for yourself an idol, whether in the form of anything that is in heaven above, or that is on the earth beneath, or that is in the water under the earth. You shall not bow down to them or worship them" (Exodus 20:3-5).

God knew our human tendency to be attracted to other gods, strange gods, new gods, and false gods. God knew that the heart can be "devious" and "perverse" (see Jeremiah 17:9) and inclined to worship idols. God knew that we could easily bargain with the culture of the day and be led astray "captive through philosophy and empty deceit, according to human tradition, according to the elemental spirits of the universe, and not according to Christ" (Colossians 2:8). God knew that our modern idols could be as dangerous, harmful, and venomous as the Canaanite, Philistine, Babylonian and other pagan idols. God knew also that when we worship such idols our lives become poorer, emptier, sadder, lonelier, and meaningless. We become blind as St. Paul put it, "The god of this world has blinded the minds of the unbelievers, to keep them from seeing the light of the gospel of the glory of Christ, who is the image of God" (2 Corinthians 4:4). No wonder St. John ended his letter with this instruction, "Little children, keep yourselves from idols" (1 John 5:21).

Idols are the enemies of our souls. They can be easy to spot like worshiping money instead of God. But they often are subtle and they look like completely harmless and even virtuous like busyness. Most of the time, they are in between like success. In any case, one would know it's an idol when it is able to insert itself between the individual and God in a way that it becomes the first concern and God becomes second, third, or much further down the line. It is also the case when we trust our own imagination, skills, power, and work more than we trust God. In this sense, we can perhaps say that all sins are, in one way or another, an expression of idolatry.

All our life, and indeed the world's life, depends on how we honestly answer the question, "Who comes first in your life and my life?" If the answer is "God," we will act in a certain way and according to certain norms. If the answer is the "idol" we worship, we will act in a completely different way and according to the idol's requirements. On the answer we honestly provide, will depend our own life, our world, and our very survival.

Here are some of the idols of the modern world we consciously or unconsciously cherish and worship.

Money and Mammon

"It's not about money," we often say. But this is precisely what it is about. It's about money—the Mammon of the New Testament and the Baal of the ancient world.

Jesus was crystal clear on this subject. He said, "No one can serve two masters; for a slave will either hate the one and love the other, or be devoted to the one and despise the other. You cannot serve God and wealth" (Matthew 6:24). In Jesus' steps, St Paul wrote: "But those who want to be rich fall into temptation and are trapped by many senseless and harmful desires that plunge people into ruin and destruction. For the love of money is a root of all kinds of evil, and in their eagerness to be rich some have wandered away from the faith and pierced themselves with many pains" (1 Timothy 6:9-10). Many other saints and wise people opted for the love of poverty rather than the love of money.

But why is money a problem? What is so special about money?

By itself money should be considered neutral. However, the love of money is not. When we become obsessed with money, when we let money run our lives, and when we become attached and addicted to it, money then becomes a dangerous commodity because it will take precedence to any other concern including the concern for God. When money is first and God is second, it becomes an idol. Jesus said, "For where your treasure is, there your heart will be also" (Matthew 6:21).

Baal—the false god of the ancient world—is still right here, right now. It is in the form of not only the "almighty" dollar, but also the form of gold, silver, yen, Euro, and more, much more. The love of money can become pervasive; one needs only to watch the TV daily news or read the daily newspapers. One would see almost on a daily basis stories of scandals, promises of strong yields, quick returns, the "you-cannot-miss-opportunity" for investment, "secure" retirement plans, robberies of all kinds including "legal" robberies, companies making billions of dollars of profit, CEOs in court for stealing customers, companies caught in falsifying products, an old woman killed for her money, and the like. If the only ends sought are efficiency and profit, one can do anything and commit any crime and without any regret or remorse in order to reach those ends. Then the only "ethical" standards of conduct that make sense are the ones that give the "freedom" to choose and justify any means that lead to the desired ends. This is not freedom. This is a mere slavery to the greed that makes us change our principles according to where the money is more abundant.

As private individuals, members of a group, or as society in general, we are all tempted by the idol of money that is pervasive and perilous and that seems to be persistent in human life. Mark Twain wrote: "Some men worship rank, some worship heroes, some worship power, some worship God, and over these ideals they dispute and cannot unite—but they all worship money."

What do you do with your money?

Money can be a blessing, but it can also be a curse. "What do you do with your money?" That is the question.

With money one can build a good and solid family house, a great school, a vast hospital, or a beautiful place of worship. Also with money one can make places of corruption, manufacture sophisticated crime machines, or construct weapons of mass destruction.

One can accumulate money thinking that the bigger the bank account, the happier one will be. One can also give money to those who do not have it, believing that this is the way to true happiness because by giving one receives.

With more money one can amplify the impact of greed, love of power, prestige, pride, indulgence, and the reign of the ego. With more money one can expand missionary works and reach out to more people in need.

With money one can darken the ways of stealing so that no one can catch the mischief. With money one can go in the dark of the night and brighten the life of someone who couldn't sleep because of hunger.

It is remarkable how Jesus condensed the situation in eight clear and simple words, "You cannot give yourself to God and money" (Matthew 6:24 NAB). So we have to choose either God or money.

Money is strange.

The truth is that money is strange, and makes people, things, and situations strange. Let money get into managements, friendships, marriages, families, religions, churches, temples, mosques, and/or any kind of relationships, and you will see how things change. With money, conflicts arise from nowhere. With money, wars are declared. With money, hospitals are built and schools are erected. Money does strange things to people. Money points to where our treasures are, and treasures reveal what our essence is; they define our identity. The things we treasure affect the way we think, speak, act, and live.

If you really want to know people in depth, give them a lot of money and see what they do with it. Then, you will certainly know who owns whom. Do we own our possessions or our possessions own us? Do we share our possessions or do we need to accumulate more because they are never enough? Do we have the capacity to appreciate something that money cannot buy or do we only make sense of the things that money can buy? Money has the power to define us. Money is strange. Beware of money.

Except perhaps for a few things, everything seems to become a business that generates money or prestige or power. We are losing little by little all that is beautiful and often seems "useless." Our mind is becoming focused on profit. Sport is becoming a huge business. Entertainment is business. Higher education is business. Even religion can become a good business. Some unhealthy individuals became very rich while appealing for helping the poor. Money was their goal and the doing good was the means to achieve that goal.

Although it is true that money is the power that allows individuals, families, communities, and world system to operate, nevertheless if we count on this power to solve all our problems, we are simply deceiving ourselves. We are just adding a bigger problem to our other problems;

"One does not live by bread alone" (Matthew 4:4). Materialism is a false answer or a shallow answer at its best. One may need sand to build a house but one cannot build a house on sand.

Money in itself is good, but not when it becomes an idol. We may use it as a blessing in order to be able to have a house, a car, food, clothes, land, etc. We may also use the money to help the least, the last, and the lost. However, we may misuse it and make it a curse to our own souls when we let into our hearts selfishness, greed, obsession with possessiveness, dishonesty, and falsehood. Who is in control of your life: God or Mammon? Who runs the show? Does success for you mean having more money? Money for what? In the kingdom of God, one is wealthy and successful when one blesses others with his or her money.

God or Mammon? Who is the one who really drives our lives? Judas had his answer to these questions.

When one mentions the topic of money, Judas is perhaps the most famous figure that comes to mind. He was the one who put money over everything else. He was driven by the love of money. Money was his top priority – his god.

On the occasion of the anointing of Jesus in Bethany, Judas saw that the precious perfumed ointment that Mary poured on Jesus' feet was a waste and it could have been given to the poor. But John, in his gospel, remarked that it was not because he was interested in the poor but "because he was a thief; he kept the common purse and used to steal what was put into it" (John 12:6). Such an attitude reached its highest point when he proposed explicitly to the chief priests: "'What will you give me if I betray him to you?' They paid him thirty pieces of silver" (Matthew 26:15). Even the "thirty pieces of silver," which is not a huge amount, will do the job.

If money is THE priority, then any amount will open the door to perform any job – even the worst one can imagine.

Then, in despair, Judas committed suicide and died, but his action of betrayal did not die with him; it continued throughout history. We still betray God. We still betray our consciences, our principles, our values, our brothers and sisters, our communities, our constituencies, and even ourselves. We do this for money. For money, we find ourselves willing to make the white black and the black white.

When money becomes the measure of everything we believe in, and we do, it becomes our god. Then we "die" for money because we live for money. We use others for money and we even send them to die in wars if those wars make us have more money.

Mammon!

Mammon is the symbol of earthly possessions and desires such as riches, greed, avarice, unjustified wealth, unjust gain, and the money that is made as an end in itself and for itself. Then the "In God we trust" becomes "In money we trust" – "the golden calf" and the controlling force and the ultimate value.

How foolish!

In seconds all our possessions can vanish. It takes one irresponsible little match to start an unstoppable fire that transforms everything into ashes. With one hurricane, one earthquake, one tsunami, one war, one act of vandalism, one riot, one gas explosion, one accident, one crash, one sophisticated robbery, one health disaster, one law suit, etc. and everything is gone.

Mammon! What happened to the Mammon we trusted?

It is an illusion to think that money makes us safe and free. Even Judas realized that money was not the solution. When he saw what a terrible thing he did, he went back into the temple and threw the 30 pieces of silver, making the coins ring as they hit the stone pavement. His money did not provide security for him, and it did not free him.

There is something else about Judas that draws attention and curiosity. This man must have been smart and above any suspicion. He must have been smart because he had been chosen to handle the money of the group, and he must have been above suspicion because no one would pick a person whose loyalty was under scrutiny and doubt. No one among the disciples dreamed that Judas had treason sentiment in his heart. But he did it. Then, only after the facts, the disciples knew it. Money and pretention can go very well together. Judas must have skillfully played the sincerity card since no one noticed that he was different from others. He looked good. He was religious like the other apostles since no one noticed he was different.

We, too, can be religious and we can accomplish all that is written in the holy books of religion, law, and tradition, and yet a Judas spirit may continue to live in us. It lives in all those who successfully play the religious game. It lives in those who religiously follow the rules, those who preach the rules, or those who enforce the rules. They do this not out of love for the rules, but for what they can gain from the rules.

The spirit of Judas lives in all those who pretend to love God before the eyes of the followers of God so that these followers become more generous in giving time and money. It lives in all those who become very rich with the money of the poor. It lives in all those who look so good in the outside but are ready to betray if more appealing interests arise.

The spirit of Judas did not die when he died. We still betray. We still give top priority to money. Every time we do that we worship Mammon, not God.

No matter how we look at the story of Judas, we find something ironic in it. This man miscalculated big time; he did not get much for his money. He might have been happy for a few moments, then what? He went back to the temple and threw the money on the ground and confessing as loudly as possible that money did not offer him the happiness and security he was craving. Then what to live for? The curse of money!

In a sense, Judas may do us a favor if his story makes us re-examine our basic loyalty to our Creator. Do we sell our Creator for "30 pieces of silver" as Judas did? Do we betray God for a better job, a better position, a better anything? Do we betray God in order to foster our greed, selfishness, and self-centeredness? Do we betray God for the "need" to be politically correct and compromise with any principle and value we hold dear? What would it take for us to sell out God? What would it take for us to create our own god that is made in our own image? Does an incognito Judas live in us, here and now? Are we the close and familiar friends who know all the ins and outs of the Master and, because of this knowledge, have a better grasp of the method of betraying? Are we the ones who are blinded by the immediate results without seeing the consequences of our actions? Are we able to successfully live a double-life and competently choose to walk the way of hypocrisy? What are our deeper motivations? What really drives our lives?

More

We all have met people who have every reason to be happy but were not. They are constantly seeking to acquire more, to accumulate more, to travel more, to do more—they seem to find some happiness in the *more* itself, forgetting that "more," by its very nature, is elusive and cannot be reached; one is continuously hungry for "more" and "more" of something. This is how some of us usually think: "I'll be happy when I buy this car or that house," or "I'll be happy when I have that promotion," or "I'll be happy when I win that game," and so it continues. And when they reach their goal, they want something else without an end in sight.

Rich people are in fact poor if, instead of focusing on their surpluses in life, they focus on their deficits—whatever they do not have yet. The "more" of everything is always needed but never reached. They are never satisfied. Greed deforms their perspective of reality.

The desire for "more" that is part of human nature, has been inflated and magnified by our culture to a degree of immense proportions and ramifications. It has impacted our lifestyles so widely that we even let "worldly" economy depend on it, and we cannot imagine that happiness is possible without it.

Take a look at the advertisements we see on TV and in magazines. Basically what they are saying is that if you want to be happy you are supposed to buy this car, this house, this shampoo, and if you have them why you don't try the new ones that just came out, and *voilà* you are the happiest person in the world. Really?! Do you still remember your birthday gift of last year? Were you happy for more than that particular evening and maybe for different reasons anyway like the opportunity, for example, of seeing family and friends together around you?

Moreover, we might think that we are more important when we have "more." So we seem to equate our self-worth with our net worth. Consequently, those who own little must count for little. No wonder we are driven by the "need" to buy things we don't necessarily need, with money we don't necessarily have, to impress people we don't necessarily like. Jesus warns about such an attitude in these terms: "Be on your guard against all kinds of greed; for one's life does not consist in the abundance of possessions" (Luke 12:15). Translation: more possessions do not make us, in God's eyes, wealthier and more qualified for the kingdom of God.

Furthermore, why do we think that the more we have, the more secure we will be? This is not obvious at all because everything we own can be taken away from us in seconds—legally or illegally—or by a natural disaster. Things cannot provide real security for us. It is not in their nature to do that. Look around and see what happened to our financial system. Can we trust our employer, our insurer, our bank account, our 401K, our portfolio, the value of our money or real estate— all our possessions—for security? Can we foresee the damages that could be left after a fire, an earthquake, a hurricane, an oil spill, a terrorist attack? Obviously we cannot.

Even though the accumulation of more things gives the impression that we could be happier, more important, and more secure, we cannot place our hope, faith, and trust in such a false god. Only before the true God should we bow and say, "Our help is in the name of the Lord, who made heaven and earth" (Psalm 124:8). The famous line of St. Augustine (354-430), "You have made us for yourself [O Lord], and our hearts are restless until they can find peace in you," proved to be true throughout the centuries and is proving to be true today more than ever.

Celebrity

By devouring our attention, our celebrity culture seems to be shaping our values and directing our concerns and actions.

But why is our culture so captivated by celebrities? What do we find in celebrities that makes them so interesting and fascinating? Why do celebrities seem to matter so much? Why do we make celebrities new gods to worship? Why are we so anxious to tell everyone we know when we see, meet, or talk to someone famous? What could be the secret of such questions?

Consciously or unconsciously we all long for significance, glory, and immortality. If we already have in some way a significant life, chances are we would feel less inclined to idolize celebrities than if we didn't have a significant life.

Celebrities have fame and seem immortal. This is exactly what we usually long for—the glory of fame and immortality. If we don't have these in ourselves, we associate ourselves with those who seem to have them. We think that this kind of connection will give us what they have. People will pay more attention to us because we know someone important. We also feel we are going to live forever because we know someone who is going to live forever.

The reality is that we don't need a celebrity to make us significant. We already are significant and we are not aware of our significance. "God sent his only Son into the world so that we might live through him" (1 John 4:9). This means that, in God's eyes—this is what really counts—we are already significant because he sent his Son for us. We "are a chosen race, a royal priesthood, a holy nation, God's own people" (1 Peter 2:9).

This is the true significance that never fades or changes. The more aware of our own significance, the less we worship the celebrity idol.

Sex

Enough! We have already been saturated. From television to movies, to live concerts, to videos, to magazines, to newspapers, to all kinds of advertisements, sex and sexuality are everywhere. Sex is available to the vacationer at the beach or family resort, the patron of the restaurant or sports event, the worker on the college campus or clubs facilities, the employee, CEO, government and even Church official. Sex is becoming a selling tool for our products; sex sells. Porn is becoming a multibillion-dollar industry. It is available in any place at any time; the Internet and the latest high tech devices seem to be proud of offering it. Sex permeates our culture and our psyche. We now confer the status of gods and goddesses on the sexiest individuals of our society. We idolize all the details of their lives. We publicize their bodily statistics. We reward them with our money and especially with our constant attention to them. We excuse their flawed lifestyles and glorify their human failures. We make the books they write about their weaknesses bestselling books. We find them "adorable" no matter what they do. "Gods" cannot do anything wrong.

Sex is becoming the thing—the god that replaces God.

But God had a better idea. God devoted an entire book of the Bible to show how sacred and poetic sex can be and how privileged and beautiful a husband and wife relationship is and should be.

Set me as seal upon your heart,
as a seal upon your arm;
for love is strong as death,
passion fierce as the grave.
Its flashes are flashes of fire,
a raging flame.
Many waters cannot quench love,
neither can floods drown it.
If one offered for love

all the wealth of one's house,
it would be utterly scorned.
(Song of Solomon 8:6-7)

When sex is enjoyed within the intensity and permanence of the marriage covenant, it becomes heavenly and godly. This is precisely how God wanted it to be. When God is God, sex is godly. When sex is god, God is absent. When God is absent, sex becomes our ticket to catastrophe.

Appearance

No matter who and what we are or where we come from—especially if we are of this Western culture—the chances are that our attitudes about our personal appearance are very high. That is because our worldly standards of youth, slimness, fitness, and external beauty are very high. Not that these are bad in themselves. No. But they would become bad if we grant them the idol status in a way that they become the only measure of truth, of the perfect living, and of the ultimate value.

How do we know that the legitimate concern with our physical appearance crossed the line of normality and simple preoccupation? The following questions could be one way to help make this distinction.

- Does our approach to physical appearance take precedence in our priorities to any other priorities and aspects of our life?

- Does our physical appearance reflect our values and qualities of our heart and soul, or is it rather a façade to cover what we are not?

- Are we happy with the amount of time we spend on our physical appearance as opposed to the amount of time we spend in praying and doing things that concern our salvation?

- Do we give the impression that our physical appearance is practically the only value that exists, and that people are attracted to us or not attracted to us, thanks to this appearance?

- Do we take too much pride in what we are wearing or using and in what these items cost?

- Do we base our self-esteem on our external self alone as if everything else is irrelevant?

- Do we think that the only way to be acceptable and accepted in society is to dress according to the latest "fashion" we can find?

- Do we disdain people who are not into the "fashion" way of life?

- Does our appearance become god and we do not know it?

No normal person wants to look old, ugly, obese, out of shape, and unhealthy. But to exalt youth, beauty, slimness, fitness, and the latest fashion in everything, in a way that these would replace God in our lives is not what God wants for us. St Paul wrote to Timothy: "The women should dress themselves modestly and decently in suitable clothing, not with their hair braided, or with gold, pearls, or expensive clothes, but with good works, as is proper for women who press reverence for God." (1 Timothy 2:9-10). The essence of what St Paul is saying is of course true for everyone—women as well as men.

We always should think in perspective. Of course we should take care of our physical conditions. But we should not spend so much time, effort, and money striving for the latest fashion in a way that allows any watcher to guess who the real god we are worshiping is. Beauty and fitness facilities are what they are, and should never become our shrines.

There is also another side of our concern for good appearance and that is the image we project of ourselves to others. In order to maintain this image we will do anything. We will lie, cover up, deny, or use all kinds of excuses, equivocations, rationalization, and even "religious" references to justify a certain reproachable conduct. We idolize our reputation and we will pay any price for it.

Furthermore, we can make a god of our way of thinking and doing things in a way that will eclipse others' ways totally and even God's way. Often we seem to be a living proof for the popular "My way or the highway" or "There are two ways of doing things: my way or the wrong way."

Success

Success can take a very subtle form of idolatry that is sometimes hard to detect. Who does not want to succeed in what he or she is doing? Can one blame a Michelangelo for the success of a "Sistine Chapel," or a Vivaldi for the success of a "Four Seasons," or a Shakespeare for the success of his plays, or an Edison for the success of his inventions, or a St. John Baptist Vianney for the success of being what a priest is supposed to be, or a St. Teresa of Calcutta for the success of her mission, or a St. Thérèse of Lisieux for the success of becoming a saint at a young age?

These successes are very good. God wants them, inspires them, and helps the individuals who carry them out to succeed in achieving the fruitful intended results. But still God is in charge in all these successes. Still God comes first.

However, there is another kind of success whose demands are without end. It is related, not to the Infinite God, but to the infinite greed we carry in us. It is OK to be Number One and be rich and famous, but not at the expense of others and by using illegal and illegitimate and unethical means. It is OK to reach our goals, provided these goals are in God's agenda. It is OK to succeed in using our potential, but not under the temptation of defining ourselves by what others think of us. It is OK to have limousines, helicopters, yachts, a big mansion, a hit television show, a thick bank account, and thousands of employees, but not to worship whatever we have. It is OK—even wonderful—to pursue our "American dream" that allows us to make it regardless of race, religion, or economic status, but not to pursue this dream *instead* of God or *ahead* of God.

In the pursuit of success we don't necessarily forget God or stop worshipping God; we simply don't give God the first place in our priorities. We have too many things to do, too many meetings to preside, too many connections to make and no energy left for prayer. We forget that the best way to stay tall is when we bow and kneel in prayer.

The pursuit of legitimate dreams and the achievement of successes—even spiritual successes such as the ministry activities and duties—can become idols if we put them *ahead* of God. We have all seen the changes that occurred to dedicated pastors, inspiring preachers, popular politicians, and hard working business men and women who were known for their honesty and integrity until the day they found success and cash. Then, they fell. "And great was [that] fall" (Matthew 7:27). If the Church is run the way one runs a very successful business firm, it wouldn't be necessarily the Church that Christ had in mind. Christ's Church is not a business. Christ is not to be bought and sold with money. Judas tried to do that one time and it was a catastrophe. True success should be based solely on what we allow God to do in us and through us.

Busyness

Gone are the days when all the members of the family and often the extended family sit down together for dinner and exchange accounts of how their days went. In those days, people seemed to have time for each other and they seemed to have time to wait for each other.

Today, we live in a much different world. Our society seems to want the mothers to work, the stores to never close, the assembly line to never stop, the TV to be "on" all the time, and the fathers to have to work over time in order to keep up with every insurance, every bill, and every unexpected expense. Moreover, almost everybody is busy talking on the telephone or text-ing or twitter-ing or browsing the Internet. No wonder we became more exposed to being exhausted, stressed out, and short-tempered. It would be nice to re-enjoy a little siesta and plan a dinner or something. But this is becoming too hard. For many of us busyness has become an idol.

But why are we so busy anyway?

There are obviously some external reasons for that. Indeed, we do have family responsibilities, job demands, social events, church duties, and the like.

There are also more profound reasons for our busyness. We may think, for example, that busyness will make us more important people since we believe, as the conventional wisdom tends to believe, that the most important people are the busiest ones.

However, our busyness can also be paradoxically a sign of laziness. This happens when we don't do our homework first by making the hard decisions. So we put forth the seemingly hard work to cover up for what we should have done before and we didn't. There is a point in what wise people usually say that only lazy people work hard.

Furthermore, many of us are busy because we don't trust that God can handle our affairs. We have a doubt that God can run things without us, pick up the pieces of today, and take care of tomorrow. Consequently we find it normal to add more and more to our schedule, believing at least unconsciously that, by doing so, we make our point clear and more manifest: we are indispensable and we doubt that God can function without our intervention.

The idol of busyness is basically related to our selfishness. Look at what Martha said to Jesus: "Lord, do you not care that *my* sister has left *me* to do all the work by *myself*? Tell her to help *me*" (Luke 10:40, emphasis is added). In our own words, we usually say something like this: "Can't you see *I'm* busy right now?" "*I* do all the work and he or she does nothing," "Can *I* have a little time just for *me*?" "*I* give and give and give, and no one seems to give anything to *me*," "*I*'ll do it *myself*; *I*'m the only one to do it right anyway."

In other words, it is all about me: my calendar, my way, my to-do lists, my priorities, my importance, my indispensability. The measure of all things is I, not anyone else, and not even God.

By stating what is really important, Jesus indicated another direction. He said: "Martha, Martha, you are worried and distracted by many things; there is need of only one thing. Mary has chosen the better part, which will not be taken away for her" (Luke 10:41-42).

What we worship is sometimes clear and obvious, even if we do not want to admit it, and sometimes it is not that clear and obvious. But what is always clear and obvious is that idolatry is more common than we might think.

8

Our Golden Calves (2)

Hypocrisy and the "Politically Correct" Lifestyle

Almost daily, reports of hypocrisy find their way into the prime-time news. Respected leaders in the community are found guilty of financial fraud or sexual misconduct. Admired sports or entertainment personalities are caught with drug possession, or domestic violence. Honorable high profile figures are noticed to be living a double life.

What is wrong with us? Why do we have trouble with authenticity? What has happened to what used to be called "authenticity," "honesty," or "integrity"?

OK! Everyone, as reality shows, has one thing or another to sell. Everyone tries to persuade others to accept his or her ideas because he or she claims to know what is true and what is not. However, real life remains, by far, more persuasive.

This is precisely what hypocrisy is all about – the failure to practice what one preaches. One will say something and do something else.

In religion as well as in the world in general, we constantly have to deal with hypocrites. Hypocrites are going to be among us as long as there is sin.

It is not uncommon that we often fail to walk the talk by not living what we preach. St. Paul—even St. Paul!—complained about this. He wrote: "I do not do the good I want, but the evil I do not want is what I do. Now if I do what I do not want, it is no longer I that do it, but sin that dwells within me" (Romans 7:19-20).

Almost daily, reports on hypocrisy fill the headlines of morning and evening news. Under the umbrella of goodness, charitable works, and all kinds of services to others, we are, at the same time, shocked by the committed fraud, sexual abuses, and other crimes and lies.

No wonder people are becoming more and more cautious and less and less trusting. Where are the days when doors of homes and cars were kept unlocked, and where are the days when people's given word was more binding than written contracts?

No wonder, why many people are becoming more selective in their relationships. Many people now seem to live by the conclusion, "Fool me once, shame on you; fool me twice, shame on me," or by the German proverb, "When the fox preaches, look to your geese."

It is strange and puzzling to see how we have become so addicted to untruth, how the discrepancy between one's actions and one's beliefs and convictions is ever expanding, and how we do too little to bring a remedy to such a disorder. We seem not to be eager to do so because of the fact that hypocrisy may provide us with some social benefits.

If dictators or rich influential individuals associate themselves with, let's say, a highly respected member of the clergy, by building a hospital or a school or an orphanage for example, those persons, without a doubt, would have done something positive for their communities, even if their "righteousness" was simply a means to hide what they did not want to show. Also, one can affect others by a kind of preaching that is not necessarily practiced by the preacher, provided that the eloquent and charismatic preacher is not caught for not walking the talk. Even an atheist can, for example, preach the commandment of not stealing to his servants or employees, because this commandment works in his or her favor. This atheist can steal from others, but others cannot steal from him or her, and this is done in the name of "morality."

Virtues are not only spiritual realities; their social pragmatic side— good or suspicious—cannot be ignored. Even during conflicts this is evident. It seems so charitable – and this is beautiful and highly recommended – to bring necessary aid to the victims of conflict and to the millions of displaced people as result of a war. But it would have been more charitable if we worked to avoid the conflict in the first place. What is worse is when we provide weapons to this side or that side or even to both sides while we are sending aid to the victims. Doesn't such an attitude smell of hypocrisy?

Furthermore, can the Christian message still be taken seriously if Christians are not better than anyone else? Why should the general population listen to them, when obvious inconsistencies exist in their own house? Should the hypocrisy of some believers be considered the fruit of faith in Christ or rather the violation of it? Should we identify the messenger with the message? Can we?

To this, St. Jerome (342-420) responds: "It is no fault of Christianity that a hypocrite falls into sin." Christians are called to live a life "worthy of the gospel of Christ" (Philippians 1:27). If they don't, that is because of sin, not because of the message. It would be a monumental error to identify Jesus' message with the way some of us live our lives.

When someone points the finger at a hypocrite believer to justify his or her own non-belief, he or she usually does this as an excuse for his or her own conduct. Jesus would say to them: "Do whatever they teach you and follow it; but do not do as they do, for they do not practice what they teach" (Matthew 23:3).

Jesus was unbelievably severe vis-à-vis the hypocrites of his time. He confronted them with harsh words:

> Woe to you, scribes and Pharisees, hypocrites!... Blind guides... blind fools... how blind you are!... You are like whitewashed tombs, which on the outside look beautiful, but

inside they are full of the bones of the dead and of all kinds of filth. So you also on the outside look righteous to others, but inside you are full of hypocrisy and lawlessness.... You snakes, you brood of vipers! How can you escape being sentenced to hell? (Matthew 23:13-33)

Jesus wanted his followers to align themselves with the truth:

Let your word be 'Yes, Yes' or 'No, No'; anything more than this come from the evil one. (Matthew 5:37)

You will know the truth, and the truth will make you free. (John 8:32)

I came to the world, to testify to the truth. Everyone who belongs to the truth listens to my voice. (John 18:37)

I am the way, and the truth, and the life. (John 14:6)

Those who do what is true come to the light, so that it may be clearly seen that their deeds have been done in God. (John 3:21)

When the Spirit of truth comes, he will guide you into all the truth. (John 16:13)

John, Paul, and James echoed what Jesus said. They wrote:

Grace and truth come through Jesus Christ. (John 1:17)

I have no greater joy than this, to hear that my children are walking in the truth. (3 John 4)

Fasten the belt of truth around your waist and put on the breastplate of righteousness. (Ephesians 6:14)

Surely you have heard about him and were taught in him, as truth is in Jesus (Ephesians 4:21)

So then, putting away falsehood, let all of us speak the truth to our neighbors, for we are members of one another. (Ephesians 4:25)

Above all, my beloved, do not swear, either by heaven or by earth or by any other oath, but let your "Yes" be yes and your "No" be no, so that you may not fall under condemnation. (James 5:12)

"The most important quality in a person connected with religion," said Albert Schweitzer, "is absolute devotion to the truth." Being devoted to the truth is not an intellectual exercise; it is, as it should be, a living reality.

Here comes the important idea of authenticity.

Authentic people are hungry for truth—truth in what they think and do and say, and truth in their way of life. They know themselves. They know their weaknesses as well as their strengths. They have their goals and they use their potential to achieve them. They live their ideals.

Authentic people keep their word. They live by "Let your word be 'Yes, Yes' or 'No, No'" (Matthew 5:37). Their word mirrors their minds and hearts.

Authentic people do not use the word "truth" as a weapon. They do not say phrases like: "I am just telling the truth," or "I am very honest, I just tell it the way it is." Under the guise of honesty, these statements can mean, "It's your fault, you blew it." People of truth do not use truth as a tool to hurt someone.

Authentic people start to be authentic with themselves first, then with another, and another, and another.

Authentic people live in the here and now. It is not that hard to live in the past or in the future. Nostalgia and reveries make us fail to experience life as it happens. *This moment* is really all that we have, and we ought to find and understand the relationship between being in the present moment and being our true selves. Guilt and preoccupation about the past as well as anxiety and worry about the future shift our focus away from the present.

But to live in the present moment does not mean to live solely by what our consciousness of the moment tells us to do, without any reference to God's will whatsoever. By being eager to harvest immediate gratification, we think that we are seeing the point of our actions. Often that's not the point at all. Authentic people do not live by the "anything goes" philosophy. Their orthodoxy has solid references. It's God, not us, who defines what is right and what is wrong.

Authentic people are not afraid, not judgmental, and not critical of themselves and others. They appreciate themselves and others and have a great sense of gratitude for their blessings and enough flexibility in managing their affairs and relationships.

Authentic people know that they are on a mission. They know their mission and they do not feel complete fulfillment until this mission is achieved. Consequently, while comfortable circumstances may give them momentary happiness, their real delight is found in being genuine, true, and committed. Authentic people find their own voices. They have their "Aha!" moment. For this moment of truth, they say, they have come. That is why they make a difference.

Authentic people know what they want and how to get it through honest and open lines of communications, straight talk, and fostering meaningful relationships with the people in their lives. They believe in what they want more than they believe in what is.

Authentic people are not deceivers. Deceivers are people who mislead; they lead others to believe something that is not true. Deceivers are self-centered; instead of pointing to God as the center of truth, they point to themselves as the way to truth. No wonder they end up distorting the truth. But, at the same time, they know how to cover up the distortion by half-truths and suitable lies.

Authentic people do not base their convictions or non-convictions on what others approve or do not approve. The gospel of John illustrates well this position. "Nevertheless many, even of the authorities, believed in [Jesus]. But because of the Pharisees they did not confess it, for fear that they would be put out of the synagogue; for they loved human glory more than the glory that comes from God" (John 12:42-43).

Authentic people are people of conscience. They do not want to succeed at the expense of truth. In a document entitled *Conscience and Truth*, Joseph Cardinal Ratzinger (who became Pope Benedict XVI) wrote: "A man of conscience, is one who never acquires tolerance, well-being, success, public standing, and approval on the part of prevailing opinion, at the expense of truth."

Authentic people place tremendous emphasis on values. These values are the solid rock that holds them steady when circumstances change and the storms hit. Values give direction to their decisions, which can be often different from what others would like. Values do not belong solely to ethics. They can be part of a correct appreciation of reality. Dietrich Bonhoeffer drew our attention to this question by saying, "'Telling the truth'... is not solely a matter of character; it is also a matter of correct appreciation of real situations and of serious reflection upon them."

Authentic people know that their experience of God grows and changes. This is why, while their beliefs remain very solid, they recognize the need and the importance of expressing the reality of God in different ways. Pope John XXIII summarized beautifully this attitude in one concise phrase. He said: "The truths preserved in our sacred doctrine can retain the same substance under different forms of expression." Authentic people are adamantly attached to the truth, but they are not afraid to express it in a new way.

Authentic people do not fear discovering who they really are. Sometimes, we fear finding out who we really are, underneath all our masks of defenses, and this causes us to resist being authentic, and to live a hypocritical life.

The cocktail of our career, money, house, position, prestige, and the like we identify with can be lost in seconds. But we still exist as we are. We should be able to say with St. Francis, "I am what I am before the Lord. Nothing else, nothing more, nothing less." When we do that, we not only reduce the intensity of the fear of being the person we might discover ourselves to be, but we will accept being who we really are, no more, no less, and not someone else. Then, we will stop chasing after external life experiences that lead to lying and wearing masks that we think might make up for our inadequacies, and we will go straight to the heart of matter—grasping the truth.

Thus, we should make every effort to really know the truth about ourselves.

The well-known phrase "Know thyself" expresses the essence of Socrates' philosophy whose real mission was to know the truth about human existence and transform men and women as moral beings. This is why he also said: "An unexamined life is not worth living."

Once we truly know ourselves, we may be able to care for ourselves. Otherwise, chances are we won't.

Self-knowledge is not an end in itself, but a road that leads to transforming a person's existence by practicing virtues such as moderation, courage, justice, intellectual consistency, compassion, and truthfulness. How can a person reach his or her full potential and live a fulfilled life if this person does not know who he or she is and what his or her purposes are?

There is a deep connection between this kind of knowing and the doing. Knowing modifies doing. There is much more at risk in knowing oneself and what is right/better and what is wrong/worse for oneself, than in, let us say, buying things or changing a career. One's whole destiny is at stake; that's the difference.

When one knows the answer to the age-old question, "Who am I?" one will start to see the truth about what really matters, about whether or not one is living the life his or her heart is longing for, and about whether or not one should find better paths to improve his or her way of being.

Failing to know oneself in depth leads to telling lies to oneself and to others.

Living a life of lies is the source of many of our greatest problems and diseases. Intimacy vanishes. Connections break up. Motivations are lost. Tension, burnout, and fatigue encroach. Respect at work disappears. Authenticity, self-esteem, and the sense of self-worth fade out. Depression and its consequences creep in.

Healthy people are honest with themselves. They tell the truth about themselves, to themselves, first. Truth does not scare them; it frees them. They search for what is real in their responses to life. They are not fulfilled otherwise.

At the age of 19, Tatiana, who was born Tajci in Croatia, became a superstar in Central Europe. Her concerts, video shoots, and personal appearances were of enormous success. She attracted huge numbers of adoring fans, especially among the young people who were looking to her for answers. But she had no answers for them. The "dream-come-true" she enjoyed did not fill the hole of emptiness and loneliness she felt in her heart. Her celebrity status was not giving her the satisfaction she wanted. She was not living her truth.

One day, at age 21, she decided to leave behind fame and glamour and all they offered, and came to the United States, alone, under a different name, and completely unknown. Anonymity, prayer, and faith brought her the freedom to find the truth about what God wanted her to be. The realization of her true self inspired her to compose music, sing about her new experiences, and share her faith in concerts in hundreds of churches.

Without a clear look at her internal truth and true self, Tatiana's other selves and unconscious desires would have continued to run the show. There is no real freedom—internal or external—without truth.

The trip into the "holy of holies" of ourselves may be painful, or an action that we often are afraid to take, but it is critical in helping to make us healthy, happy, and holy. Truth will turn a person into a truthful one.

In the "holy of holies" of our being, "We are not who we know ourselves to be," wrote Henri J. M. Nouwen beautifully, "but who we are known to be by God." Explaining more, he said:

> We are not what we can acquire and conquer, but what we have received. We are not the money we earn, the friends we make, or the results we achieve; rather, we are who God made us in God's infinite love. As long as we keep running around anxiously trying to affirm ourselves or be affirmed by others, we remain blind to the One who has loved us first, dwells in our heart, and is indeed our true self.

Some of the masks we put on are known to us. But the majority of them are unconscious creations. There is no better place to learn how to take them all off, and get rid of them, than in the home-ness and safety of the body of Christ. It is crucial to understand ourselves from God's point of view, not ours. Here are some of the lies we, knowingly or unknowingly, say about ourselves and the truth that God wants us to live by:

UNTRUTH	TRUTH
I am worthless.	"Then God said, 'Let us make humankind in our image, according to our likeness'" (Genesis 1:26).
I feel defeated and paralyzed.	"For God did not give us a spirit of cowardice, but rather a spirit of power and of love and of self-discipline" (2 Timothy 1:7).

"But thanks be to God, who gives us the victory through our Lord Jesus Christ" (1 Corinthians 15:57)

I'll always fail and I'll never change.

"I can do all things through him who strengthens me" (Philippians 4:13).

"The Lord will fulfill his purpose for me" (Psalms 138:8).

Walking in the truth does not seem to give me results.

"The one who is righteous will live by faith" (Galatians 3:11).

God is not going to keep forgiving me.

"If we confess our sins, he who is faithful and just will forgive us our sins and cleanse us from all unrighteousness" (1 John 1:9).

I feel overwhelmed, and like I am losing my mind.

"Those of steadfast mind you keep in peace—in peace because they trust in you" (Isaiah 26:3).

I don't feel I am standing on solid ground.

"Trust in the Lord forever, for in the Lord God you have an everlasting rock" (Isaiah 26:4).

I quit. Who cares? Does God care?

"Be steadfast, immovable, always excelling in the work of the Lord, because you know that in the Lord your labor is not in vain" (1 Corinthians 15:58).

God won't use me if I'm not strong.

"My grace is sufficient for you, for power is made perfect in weakness. So, I will boast all the more gladly of my weaknesses, so that the power of Christ may dwell in me" (2 Corinthians 12:9).

To be accepted, I have to be perfect.	"If we say that we have no sin, we deceive ourselves, and the truth is not in us" (1 John 1:8).
I constantly look for others' approval.	"Am I now seeking human approval, or God's approval? Or am I trying to please people? If I were still pleasing people, I would not be a servant of Christ" (Galatians 1:10).
Everybody's doing it.	"You shall not follow a majority in wrongdoing" (Exodus 23:2).
What is the point in telling the truth when everybody lies.	"I do my best always to have a clear Conscience toward God and all people" (Acts 24:16).
No one loves me.	"I have loved you with an everlasting love" (Jeremiah 31:3).

God's word is not something we passively listen to or read on a page. God's word is powerful. It forms and shapes our understanding as Christians. It defines our identity as human beings from God's point of view. It generates life, produces change, cleanses minds, heals hurts, builds characters, nourishes souls, and causes fulfillment. James pointed out, "In fulfillment of his own purpose he (the Father of lights) gave us birth by the word of truth, so that we become a kind of first fruits of his creatures" (James 1:18). One can die not only from hunger, but also from junk food. This is why one should count on no other but the word of God for true nourishment.

The Scripture was not given to us to increase our knowledge of God—although this is what it does too. The Scripture was given to us to transform our lives (see 2 Corinthians 3:18) radically by making of us loving people. Love defines us as it defines God.

In the body of Christ, the greatest commandment is to love God with all our hearts and minds, and to love others as ourselves. Love makes others feel safe. The safer they feel, the less their need for masks as mechanisms for self-protection.

When we know the truth about ourselves as children of God, and we know the truth of God's love for us—which is a fundamental truth of our identity—and that love is to reach others, we show them that we are Christ to them as they are Christ to us. Now that's even beyond simple transparency. "Now the Lord is the Spirit, and where the Spirit of the Lord is, there is freedom" (2 Corinthians 3:17). What a realization!

The real miracle that transforms our lives is when we turn to God to ask the question of the secret of our being, and we hear the answer in quiet intimacy: "You are my beloved children."

Being a "beloved child of God" is the miracle truth that is at the base of every imaginable fulfillment and cure of any malaise.

Our general well-being and health are dependent upon seeing the truth that we are the beloved children of God. Jesus told us, "The eye is the lamp of the body. So, if your eye is healthy, your whole body will be full of light; but if your eye is unhealthy, you whole body will be full of darkness" (Matthew 6:22-23). Do we have healthy eyes to see our truth in God? Don't we know that we are not what others say we are, but what God says we are?

Finding our identity in God is, therefore, critical for our general well-being. This truth frees us from the need of others' approval to define us, from the urgency of any kind of possessions or power to describe our essence, and from the obligation to meet the expectations of our society to live our true purpose in life. The truth is that we are citizens of the kingdom of God and we live by the golden rule of the kingdom, which is love.

In the kingdom of God, logical principles and ideologies do not work if they are not in concert with love, because reality itself is grounded in God, and God is love, not an abstract concept or a logical system. That is why living by just principles does not always lead to truth. Love always does. Love is the basis for the ability of perceiving the truth in its essence in all aspects of life.

God is "the way, and the truth, and the life" (John 14:6) and "God is love" (1 john 4:16). Any other understanding of God is a deformed mental exercise and a bad hypocritical practice. One can make a very good living with a "politically correct" lifestyle, but one cannot make a life.

The Repeated lies

"A lie told often enough becomes the truth," was believed to have been said by Vladimir Lenin. William James said something similar: "There's nothing so absurd that if you repeat it often enough, people will believe it." Indeed, in our ordinary lives, especially in matters of politics and religion, lies are so powerful that they may create reality.

Are we surprised if we see some people, especially among our leaders and politicians, lie to us almost constantly, persistently, and repeatedly? Are we surprised if we see a good number of them living a double life – one life for you and me for the show and support, and the other one for them to hide in the secret of evasiveness and darkness?

Here we should not generalize because we still have, thank God, people who still believe in integrity and honesty. However, it is fair to say that the majority of us have adopted the "politically correct" doctrine that allows the use of any means, honest or not, in order to reach a projected goal. Believe it or not, politics and religion seem to offer the most fertile ground for lies and bad behaviors.

Truth is the first casualty of modern life.

Truth can be the first and most recognizable casualty of modern life. If we no longer know what a lie is, chances are that's because we no longer know what truth is. One of the most telling illustrations of this fact is our modern wars and how our corporate media's coverage describes the events. The old saying, "The first casualty of war is the truth" is so true. Do we really know why we went to this or that war? Do we really know who broke the cease-fire first? Do we really know how many people were killed from both sides? Do we really know who became very rich as a result of this or that conflict? Add to this all the other questions you may have in your mind. But, this we seem to certainly know and agree on that "The first casualty of war is the truth."

Apart from a few exceptions—thank God for these good exceptions—our conversations, behaviors, and relationships in general unfortunately do not inspire trust. How privileged and lucky you are if you can say you have never been lied to! Do you know anyone who has never been lied to? Personally, I have not met that person yet.

Truth is one of the first casualties of our modern life. The question "Is it true?" has become, it is sad to say, "Whose truth is it?" People tend to live by their beliefs, even if their beliefs are not true.

Practically, truth seems to have lost its correlation with reality to become a mere plausibility or especially an effort to obtain a certain desired effect. It is mainly used to confirm an agenda or carry out a mission. We no longer discover truth; we create the truth that is in our image. We easily twist our perceptions and make our opponents look bad in order to promote ourselves and meet our needs and interests. While refusing to acknowledge any valid truth in the other side's position, we monopolize the right to truth as if "the doctrine of infallibility" has moved to our side, and as if we were immune to flaws, inconsistencies, and shortsightedness.

No wonder we've made our world a world of spin, bias, and a well established excessive relativism.

Yet, in the heart of our hearts, we know that, without truth, nothing is worth living or dying for. This is why the pursuit of truth has been, still is, and will ever be a widely shared project of humankind. There is and will always be an urgent need for people of truth. We know there is no other way to live freely and be fully human.

But if, in the depth of our hearts, we greatly love and appreciate truth, why then do we lie almost spontaneously? Why does the epidemic of cheating cover all segments of society? Why are we so apathetic in the face of hypocrisy? More importantly, how can we free ourselves from lies to become men and women of truth?

Strangely and paradoxically, we seem to live in a tell-all culture. We are free to confess our feelings, our frustration, our shyness, our failures, our indiscretions, and our struggles to wake up and go on with our lives.

Yet, politicians lie to get elected, doctors lie on reports, scientists fabricate data, professionals and experts distort facts and events, CEOs of corporations cook the books, journalists twist news, universities lie about athletes, advertisers lie about products, ordinary citizens lie on income tax returns, and pastors lie about money and private life. In all these cases, truth is so stretched that reality is recognizable no more, and cheating becomes the common currency that is justified by an "everybody's-doing-it" rationale. Consequently, there is no surprise in seeing ourselves immersed in various forms of equivocation, cover-up, camouflage, delusion, complicity of inaction, and—even worse—we try to mitigate any attempt for accountability from and to anyone.

Don't you think we clearly are out of alignment with what is good, true, right, and real? What is wrong with us? Why do we need to lie in the first place?

Why do we lie?

In the thesauruses, we see the word "lie" synonymous with falsehood, untruth, delusion, perjury, duplicity, insincerity, deceitfulness, phoniness, fallaciousness, simulation, hypocrisy, dishonesty, prevarication, distortion, fabrication, false pretense, sham, and more. This is enough to convince us about the extension and forms of lies we consciously or unconsciously can be guilty of in our daily lives.

A few years ago, authors James Paterson and Peter Kim conducted an interesting survey, which went beyond the superficial five-minute poll, about private morals and values. This study was published in a book called *The Day America Told the Truth*. What they found is astonishing. For example:

Lying has become an integral part of the American culture, a trait of the American character. We lie and don't even think about it. We lie for no reason. The writer Vance Bourjaily once said, "Like most men, I tell a hundred lies a day." That's about right. And the people we lie to most are those closest to us.

Just about everyone lies—91 percent of us lie regularly.

Americans are making up their own rules, their own laws. In effect, we're all making up our own moral codes. Only 13 percent of us believe in all of the Ten Commandments. Forty percent of us believe in five of the Ten Commandments. We choose which laws of God we believe in. There is absolutely no moral consensus in this country as there was in the 1950s, when all our institutions commanded more respect. Today, there is very little respect for the law—for any kind of law.

Yesterday's verities had vanished. Unpredictability and chaos became the norm.

If these findings are true, and if what a TV preacher once said, "The average person lies about 200 times a day" is true, we do not have a pretty picture of ourselves at all. Isn't this the picture of an ethical disarray—a jungle?

The problem of lying is obviously not the monopoly of one special country, or one special culture, or one special ethnic group, or one special religion, or one special time in history. Look, for example, how philosopher Simone Weil (1909-1943) warned her fellow-citizens in France, "We live in an age so impregnated with lies that even the virtue of blood voluntarily sacrificed is insufficient to put us back on path of truth" Paul wrote to the Colossians, "Do not lie to one another" (Colossians 3:9). Aristotle warned, "All that one gains by falsehood is not to be believed when he speaks the truth."

Why in the world do we seem to have difficulty telling the truth? Here we do not have a shortage of reasons.

A first reason is that we might be guilty of a bigger failure and want to hide it. Lying, which we consider a lesser evil, becomes a way of self-protection. Therefore, we lie for security reasons.

A second reason is the reason of character. When lies become habits, they also become character. It does not take long to be known as a chronic liar, in which case we lose hold of the truth by believing our own lies. Also, sometimes we lie because we can lie for the fun of it, and to get away with it and not be caught. Fyodor Dostoevsky (1821-1881) wrote:

> When we lie to ourselves, and believe our own lies, we become unable to recognize truth, either in ourselves or in anyone else, and we end up losing respect for ourselves and for others. When we have no respect for anyone, we can no longer love, and, in order to divert ourselves, having no love in us, we yield to our impulses, indulge in the lowest forms of pleasure, and behave in the end like an animal, in satisfying our vices. And it all comes from lying—lying to others and ourselves.

A third reason is that repeated lies, which give the appearance of success, help liars to become more accomplished in the "craft" of lying. They become experts in lying.

A fourth reason is that we can, in order to justify our conduct, rationalize and give explanations for any behavior we choose, even though in our heart we do not believe what we are saying. One obvious justification for our conduct, we think, is the use of the polls and statistics. "80 percent do this or that," we say. But we forget that truth has nothing to do with majority, minority, or even unanimity. This is not its language. The earth was revolving around the sun even when we were saying the opposite.

A fifth reason is that by substituting living-the-lie to living-in-the-truth, we not only turn any sense of morality upside down, but we think that it is our job—a proof of loyalty—to do this for the good of the company or administration we work for. In this sense, we think that lies pay or promise to pay.

Loyalty to a company, a community, or a country should never blind us from seeing the truth. Even though loyalty is certainly a wonderful quality, we should seek truth first, because loyalty can cover many sins and crimes. Dorothy Day pointed out rightly: "Our job is not to look for results but to be faithful for the truth." Therefore, results should flow from the truth, not the truth from results.

Furthermore, we are always tempted to adapt and adjust facts to what our superiors would like to see and hear, and we turn, as they do, the blind eye to what they do not want to see. Some of us are becoming so skilled in lying that we are no longer "amateur," but real "professional." Obviously, certain careers, more than others, count heavily on such skills.

A sixth reason is to set for oneself unrealistic goals and unreachable ideals. These goals and ideals can certainly be good in themselves. But they can also constitute an effective tactic of falsehood when we set them so high that they cannot be reached.

A seventh reason is that, in order to advance an ideology or a certain agenda of any kind, we tend to create a persona of ourselves. The Latin word "persona" means "a mask." We want to wear a mask, and act differently from who and what we are, to improve on ourselves. Our world, which counts heavily on first impressions, encourages us to "sell ourselves on sight." In such a world, depth becomes less important than appearance, honesty less significant than "face-value," and truth less attractive than winning lies. This is why we do not hesitate to go to plastic surgeons, implant hair, spin résumés, twist events, and over-inflate our capacities. Such makeovers are seen today as a normal road to advancement in life, rather than a handicap.

An eighth reason is that we may wear a mask for latent motives. Maybe there is some part (perhaps the deepest part) about ourselves that we rather not reveal openly, or perhaps we fear to confront ourselves.

Maybe we are not sure what it is either. Our unconscious can be a warehouse for repressed truths we have difficulty facing. In this context, Plato talked about *Appetite*, Freud about *Id*, Nietzsche about *Dionysus*, and Jung about *Shadow*. Is it not Socrates' intent for us to get rid of the mask we wear and reveal ourselves at least to ourselves? His famous dictum "Know thyself" of about 2400 year ago is more needed than ever in modern times. We do not love ourselves, and we do not know that we do not love ourselves. It seems that no matter what we do, it is not enough. A lie, we think, can cover up for this deep empty hole of dissatisfaction and the need to be loved. A lie may attract attention to us—the attention we desperately are looking for. We need to know the truth about ourselves, but we don't.

Do our troubles with truth mean that there is no truth?

Truth exists whether we like or not.

Do not believe those who tell you that truth does not exist. Why should you believe them if what they are saying is not true anyway, since they just said there was no truth? For a while, their "truth" may serve them well, socially, financially, and even "religiously." Counting on cunning compromises and on wearing appropriate masks is not the way to the fullness of life; truth is.

It is in the nature of truth, not to move according to the world, but to move the world. A person of truth refuses to be edited by society. A person of truth leaves the greatest impact on his or her society.

Do we know who we truly are? Our very lives, more than our words, are the answer to this age-old question.

If we are created in the image of God, only in God do we discover the truth about ourselves. Christianity is not knowledge about God; it is knowledge in God. God is love. We are unable to know this truth except by, in, and with love. In *The Cloud of Unknowing,* an enduring classic of Christian spirituality that was written in the fourteenth century, we read: "By love God may be caught and held: by thinking never." This is how critical was the "[Having] the mind of Christ" (1 Corinthians 2:16) of

Paul. God knows about ourselves more than we, ourselves, know about ourselves. God created us for love.

Truth is truth when it is according to God's plan, and to the way the divine plan is unfolding. Our own individual destiny as well as the whole destiny of humankind is christological in essence. That's the truth. Aren't we in the image of God? Therefore, a transfiguration in Christ should be expected. God's grace is available. How we are going to respond to it remains to be seen. Maximus the Confessor (580-662) says: "See how the Lord has given us the power to become eternally the children of God; henceforth our salvation is in our will."

The age of the complexities of life in which we live needs to capture God's truth—the truth that transforms and heals souls, minds, hearts, and bodies. Since we cannot be "know-it-all" and have "black and white" knowledge of everything, we need a north star or a certain map to guide us in our struggles with reality. Dr. M. Scott Peck offers a helpful image:

The less clearly we see the reality of the world—the more our minds are befuddled by falsehood, misperceptions, and illusions—the less able we will be to determine correct courses of action and make wise decisions. Our view of reality is like a map with which to negotiate the terrain of life. If the map is true and accurate, we will generally know where we are, and if we have decided where we want to go, we will generally know how to get there. If the map is false and inaccurate, we generally will be lost.

God's word is that north star and that map. Only God's word is true and absolute, yesterday, today, and forever (see Hebrews 13:8). Only this truth gives true freedom. The rest is truth telling, concept shifts, and human fluctuations. If it does not make reference to God, any system we create, with the hope that it will help in the betterment of the world, will sooner rather than later collapse under its deceptions and lies, bringing more miseries to humankind. This is also the truth. A system or a state may provide some dignity to a person. But only God makes every person a person of dignity.

Mystics and saints often used silence instead of speech to express truth. They knew that silence—the gaps in the midst of a speech—is essential for a communication to work. Their lives were more eloquent than the limitations of language, to bear witness to the truth. They lived truth. They lived it in words, and especially in between the words—in the eloquent silence that gives meaning to the words. To do so was not, is not, and will never be, an easy task. Apart from a few exceptions, a person of truth often pays a high price for witnessing to the truth, because neither the right nor the left knows where to classify him or her. Truth is not subject to classifications and limitations.

Truth is a set journey toward the one who said, "I am the way, and the truth, and the life" (John 14:6). It is the way toward the Way that leads to true Life. It is the truth that transforms profoundly and radically, because it sets everything it touches on fire—the fire of the Holy Spirit.

Integrity calls people to know who they truly are, be at home with their true selves, and shape the world in their image which is a reflection of the image of God. By closely following Christ, one does not go astray, as mystic and theologian Richard of St. Victor (d. 1173) suggested: "If you are in a hurry to reach higher things, you will go safely if truth goes ahead of you. Without truth your labour is in vain. Truth does not want to deceive, and so it cannot be deceived. If you do not want to go astray, follow Christ." When we follow Christ, we start to see as God sees. Here, Meister Eckhart (1260-1328), one of history's great mystics, cannot help but say unambiguously:

It is your destiny to see as God sees,
to know as God knows,
to feel as God
feels.
How is this possible? How?
Because divine love cannot defy its very self....

Every object, every creature, every man, woman and child
has a soul and it is the destiny of all,
to see as God sees, to know as God knows,
to feel as God feels, to Be
as God
is.

So, a repeated lie does not make it truth. It is truth that makes a lie, a "true" lie. That is the truth.

Not telling the truth is only one way of lying. The other way is lying with our very lives.

Complacency

Beware of complacency; it is a killer. It will kill your relationship with family and others. It will kill your marriage. It will kill your relationship with God. As indifference, not hate, is the opposite of love, complacency, not death, is the opposite of life.

Toxic complacency!

Dictionary.com defines complacency as *"a feeling of quiet pleasure or security, often while unaware of some potential danger, defect, or the like; self-satisfaction or smug satisfaction with an existing situation, condition, etc."* Elsewhere, complacency was described as follows:

Complacency is a blight that saps energy, dulls attitudes, and causes a drain on the brain. The first symptom is satisfaction with things as they are. The second is rejection of things as they might be. "Good enough" becomes today's watchword and tomorrow's standard. Complacency makes people fear the unknown, mistrust the untried, and abhor the new. Like water, complacent people follow the easiest course – downhill they draw false strength from looking back. (Anonymous)

Complacency usually comes in two forms: self-satisfaction and self-defeat.

We have people who are at ease, self-satisfied, comfortable with the things as they are, and they feel no need for improving to the status quo. Because of their concentration on worldly pleasure and comfort, they seem blind or they pretend to be blind to the decay in society. In such a case, they will certainly be disturbed by any newness, freshness, renewal, and aliveness. A genuine and non-complacent religious person knows that God is calling him or her to something bigger than the current situation.

We also have people who feel self-defeated, overwhelmed by their difficult circumstances, depressed, tired of it all, and ready to give up. They tend to justify such an attitude by the "Why bother since nothing is going to change anyway?" attitude.

Most of us may experience, from time to time, some kind of complacency. The real problem, however, takes place when complacency becomes a way of life. Such a phenomenon was described this way:

It [complacency] invades areas once occupied by our passion, interest, desire, and focus. When complacent, the valued things that had captivated our thoughts, hearts, and energies tend to fade from priority and can even become mundane or the boring routine of everyday life. Burnout in our work life, loss of fire in relationships, and the lack of zeal for things we once held important are common experiences. The shame is not in complacency but in the failure to recognize it and take corrective measures to regain our footing. (Anonymous)

The Titanic is often remembered as an example of complacency. We built a ship with the most up-to-date technology available and we declared the ship as unsinkable. The ship carried life boats for 33% of the people who were on board. The "good enough" conviction and the special narcotic drug called "pride" led to the loss of 1500 lives.

The first symptom of complacency is the satisfaction with the status quo and the things as they are. The second symptom is the rejection of any improvement and of the things as they might be and must be. This means that each day is supposed to be a new day for growth and development. But, instead, we choose stagnation.

It takes energy and purposefulness to live a life without complacency. We lose that fire within, that once burned bright, when we are too busy, not busy enough, fatigued, bored, and especially when we take a partner or God for granted. Then, slowly and little by little, complacency sets in. We still do the work -- duties and rituals – but love is gone. We run from someone (God, a spouse, a friend) to something (church activities, jobs, grades, investments...). What was once first, now becomes last. What was a priority now no longer is. We, then, exhibit an attitude of self-sufficiency which shows no real personal need for any relationship with God or with anybody. We think we can handle life and what it brings by ourselves without the need of others or of God. We believe that constant dependence on others and on God is not part of reality. It is rather an imaginary need. When we don't think about God, everything ends up being about "me," my own comfort, my own well-being, and my own realistic or unrealistic desires.

Complacency reveals that we are comfortable in the culture in which we live. When we align ourselves too closely with the philosophical systems and the lifestyles of the day, we lose the spiritual and critical evaluation of these things. We become contented with the status quo instead of becoming vitalized and invigorated by the kingdom of God and its promises. When we are too settled in the lower, we stop striving for the higher.

Complacency is a sin against hope. It says there is no longer hope for a change. When we no longer have intimacy with God, when we are no longer part of God's purpose, and when we lose our motivation for making of this world the kingdom of God, we, in fact, declare that we cannot change anything and that God is not involved in the world he created. This is a sin against God because we think he is not doing anything, and against us because we think that we are not able to change anything. We may still say "In God We Trust" but we no longer mean it.

In spiritual life, there is no such a thing called status quo; either we go forward or we find ourselves going backward. If we get complacent, we may find that we have become lukewarm and further from God than we want to be. Here is the clear warning:

> I know your works; you are neither cold nor hot. I wish that you were either cold or hot. So, because you are lukewarm, and neither cold nor hot, I am about to spit you out of my mouth. For you say, 'I am rich, I have prospered, and I need nothing.' You do not realize that you are wretched, pitiable, poor, blind, and naked.... Be earnest, therefore, and repent. (Revelation 3:15-17, 19)

God invites us to know more (it is impossible to completely know the Ultimate), to be more (our world is in desperate need of saints), and to do more (choosing to put others' need ahead of own). God wants us to love, and we often choose to be pious over loving. Somehow we find it simpler to be devoted than to be compassionate. We find it easier to read books on prayer or talk about prayer than to really pray. It could be more comfortable to find refuge in rituals and rules than to engage in the uncharted wisdom of love. No matter how hard we try to put God in the box of our theologies, philosophies, and the other sciences and disciplines, God is new everyday and cannot be reduced to our so limited understanding. God is love and love has no limits. To think that we have arrived is a trap. Love requires an unceasing passion that rejects the lukewarmness of complacency.

There is often complacency within religious institutions. The fact that some institutions, while doing well with their programs of social reforms and spiritual activities, for example, are unconcerned with the very word of God and personal holiness, constitutes another example of complacency. We may think we are OK with God, but have we ever considered and pondered what God has to say about us? Complacency can be a subtle cause of apostasy from God throughout time without being aware of it.

God wants to get to the roots of our dysfunction. God wants the total renovations of our lives and he is not pleased by just performing philanthropic acts. Dustin Moskovitz says: "There's a lot of complacency in philanthropy. People figure organizations are trying to do good, and that's enough, even if the results aren't there. But that's wasteful and inefficient. It crowds out better programs." Francis Spufford is even more direct when he says: "Christians are as subject to complacency as anybody else, and we can certainly settle into repetition and forget that something radical and extraordinary is being asked of us as well - that we hold to an extraordinary promise about how, from moment to moment, something enters the world and enters us, after which everything is different."

Being complacent with our situations and resigned to our fate is not what God wants for our lives. God wants us to align ourselves with the truth, do what is right, and be a blessing for others. God wants us to be a living proof of his existence.

"The only thing necessary for the triumph of evil," said Edmund Burke, "is for good people to do nothing." These words can apply in every aspect of our lives. They apply in politics, in social justice and peace, in the struggle for freedom, in cultural scientific pursuits, and the development and the environment. They also apply in our relationships with others and with God.

Evil triumphs when good people do nothing and remain silent. Such an attitude is not only complacency but also complicity; this is exactly what the enemy wants; to be happy with the status quo and remain silent.

Silence is good and recommended when centered, meditative, and focused on physical, mental, and spiritual health. But it is detrimental before injustice, violence, sin, and all violations of the dignity and rights of humanity. Then it is the efficient contributor and accomplice in the expansion of evil. This is exactly what the enemy wants.

Complacency is not our ally but the enemy's ally.

Compromise

We do compromise. When we don't, we usually let the "My way or the highway" run the show. Sometimes we even go much further than that.

When real dialogue is not possible and when any hope for compromise vanishes, aggressive behaviors usually happen including a possible annihilation of those who dare to oppose us.

Therefore, compromise is a great tool for making peace between people. It allows a convenient accommodation with others who co-exist under the same roof, in the same town, in the same group, in the same nation, and in the same world.

It is normal to have different opinions since we have different backgrounds and ethnicities, different religions and traditions, and different cultures and ideologies. Therefore, it is normal that we don't think in the same way, we don't see the world in the same way, and we don't act in the same way. But we need to live in the same world. So, we compromise. From a human point of view it cannot be otherwise, because no one can pretend to have the truth, the whole truth, and nothing but the truth. Consequently, compromise is good for us; our very survival may depend on it.

However, this is not the whole story.

It is a fact that a few of us compromise in the secondary matters of life, but not in the essential. It is also a fact that a good majority of us always feel ready to compromise in any circumstance and for any reason, and in secondary matters as well as in the essential. By doing so, we think we are pleasing everyone and then everyone will be happy and will love us. But, as the reality shows, this is not so.

The ancient Greek storyteller Aesop wrote a fable to prove that people who desire to make everyone happy will end up having no real friends, after all. Please read with me this little fable entitled *The Birds, the Beasts and the Bat*:

Many years ago, the birds and the beasts declared war against each other. No compromise was possible, and so they went at it tooth and claw.

It was a terrible battle. Many a hare and many a mouse died. Chickens and geese fell by the score -- and the victor always stopped for a feast.

Now the bat had not openly joined either group as he did not want to be caught on the losing side. So when the birds asked which side he was on the bat quickly replied, "I have wings, I am on your side of course." And when the beasts asked who he supported, the bat responded, "with my sharp teeth and fur, it is obvious I am on the side of the beasts." The truth of it was that he did little to help either group spending most of his time telling tales about the other.

When the battle was over, the conduct of the bat was discussed at the peace conference. The birds and beasts all turned angrily against the bat when they realized how many times the bat had changed sides and spread rumors.

Since then the bat lives in fear of the beasts and the birds -- hiding in dark towers and deserted ruins, flying out only in the night.

Living in the dark, as the fable suggests, is the downside of compromise.

People of compromise do not like the light, so they hide in deserted corners. They prefer ambiguity, half-truths, and empty promises. They are everywhere on the map. Obscurity is their strategy and a vague answer is their tactic. They are people of principles if necessary, and they are not people of principles if necessary also. They follow a particular ideology, and they don't. They are members of this or that religion, and they are not. They are with this or that policy, and they are not. They are very loyal, and they are not. They are your friends, and they are not. It all depends on the winds of the moment and the different circumstances.

But when are we allowed to compromise and when are we not allowed? Why do we compromise in the first place?

Sometimes we compromise for material gain. Sometimes we compromise because of family ties and biased friendship loyalty. Some other times we compromise out of fear, and in other times we compromise because of our desire to avoid confrontation. Furthermore, we compromise because of the lack of faith, and that is the most dangerous of all. We may have a good heart and the noblest of intentions for saying and doing the right things, but if we compromise with the truth, "it won't work." Our mind does not create God. God exists whether we believe it or not.

God is a God of absolutes and God is by far much bigger than all that we are able to understand and imagine.

But many of us prefer relativism. One of today's mantras would be "You have your God and I have mine." That's for today, tomorrow is tomorrow. Here, most of us are very good "politicians." Politicians often change their position based on the political risks and interests. It all depends on that particular audience they are speaking to. Then, truth depends on circumstances.

This is precisely how compromise leads to deceit, legalism, ambiguity, procrastination, and dysfunction. Then a hypocritical double-life style would become accepted as the new normal, and it would be justified as "not so bad after all" and "everybody does it and it is not the end of the world."

Compromise. Compromise. Compromise. We live in an age of compromise. Politicians compromise to secure votes. Police compromise to avoid riots. Employers compromise to prevent employees from unionizing. Everyone is welcome. Every opinion is accepted. Every fashion is tolerated. Every lifestyle is authorized. Every behavior is allowed. Every way of expressing oneself or even worshiping is permitted. The distinction between what is right and what is wrong is broken down, and there isn't a right or a wrong way to do things. Only the "politically correct" way counts. We do compromise and we concede an inch here and an inch there, and a half-truth here and a half-truth there, following the path of least resistance. The spirit of the age seems to have taken over by pressing us to accept and live by the standards this world accepts and lives by. More and more we tend to be like everyone else of this culture. We want to say what they say, think what they think, wear what they wear, act like they act, and live the way they live. Somehow we are becoming afraid to be different. Compromise. Compromise. Compromise.

Nothing will pervert one's spiritual vision more than a spirit of compromise. It has the capacity to turn light into darkness and darkness into "light." The compromising teacher of truth will become, sooner rather than later, a disgrace and a detriment to the cause he or she has espoused. The very truth that is presented in a compromised way becomes a cause of rejection for the one that was supposed to embrace that truth. God himself will be disregarded when God is conceived and presented in a compromised way.

Take another look to what the "old farmer" used to say: "God said it. I believe it. That settles it." Is this *passé*? If this is so, how one would explain:

You must neither add anything to what I command you nor take away anything from it, but keep the commandments of the Lord your God with which I am charging you. (Deuteronomy 4:2)

Every word of God proves true… Do not add to his words, or else he will rebuke you, and you will be found a liar. (Proverbs 30:5, 6)

For truly I tell you, until heaven and earth pass away, not one letter, not one stroke of a letter, will pass from the law until it is accomplished. (Matthew 5:18)

See to it that no one takes you captive through philosophy and empty deceit, according to human tradition, according to the elemental spirits of the universe, and not according to Christ. For in him the whole fullness of deity dwells bodily, and you have come to fullness in him, who is the head of every ruler and authority. (Colossians 2:8-10)

Modern science, theology, philosophy, psychology, and history contribute greatly in the understanding of a text. Who is going to doubt that? But any interpretation seems like a compromise when it tends to harmonize with the spirit of the world more than it does with the very word of God. In any case, science should not supersede Scripture, experience should not substitute for doctrine, and pragmatism should not dominate theology.

When it comes to the world of God, one cannot compromise. Accommodations and concessions are not the language that God uses, and they don't make anyone happy. The psalmist described the way by saying: "Happy are those whose way is blameless, who walk in the law of the Lord. Happy are those who keep his decrees, who seek him with their whole heart, who also do no wrong, but walk in his ways. You have commanded your precepts to be kept diligently" (Psalm 119:1-4).

No one is perfect, but making a mistake and failing to reach perfection is not the same as compromising convictions, attitudes, and lifestyles.

The compromiser who tries to live in two worlds got shot at from both sides. It is not a good place to be.

"Whoever is not with me is against me, and whoever does not gather with me scatters" (Matthew 12:30), said the Lord.

Indifference

Indifference is one of the favorite ways for evil to conquer the world.

Indifference deeply impacts our lives whether we know it or not, and whether we want to admit or not. Most of the time, it makes a bad difference with unfortunate consequences, and then we cry out, "Wolf!" when we were not supposed to "lie," in the first place. We blame the consequences and we forget what led us to them, pretending that we have done all that was possible in those particular circumstances.

Indifference is not indifferent. There is no such a thing that is called "indifferent" or "no difference."

When we utter the word "indifference," many synonymous words rush to mind, words like apathy, unconcern, disinterest, insouciance, nonchalance, unresponsiveness, detachment, dispassion, unimportance, insignificance, irrelevance, mediocrity, aloofness, withdrawal, emotionlessness, impassiveness, numbness, passiveness, nonchalance, and more. All of these words, when applied in human context, prove the adequacy of George Bernard Shaw's line, "The worst sin towards our fellow creatures is not to hate them, but to be indifferent to them: that's the essence of inhumanity."

This happens when indifference means "no difference." Then there is no difference between light and darkness, peace and violence, good and evil. Now we can look the other way, pretending not to have seen, or heard of, or known.

The secret power of indifference is part of what we call weapons of mass destruction because it has the capacity to kill the masses too. Don't the books of history prove it? How many genocides happened in even most recent times, and we looked the other way? The worst part is when we knowingly or unknowingly create the appropriate conditions for a crime to happen, and then we just wash our hands declaring our innocence. We look the other way, or we cry out, "Wolf!" when we are the first ones to have caused it.

We cannot say, for example, there is "no difference" in whatever our children learn in school, whatever they watch on TV, whatever they read in books and magazines, and whatever connection they choose to have with others in real life or on the Internet. If "everything goes" because we become indifferent to what is going on, we implicitly are allowing undesired consequences to happen. Sooner or later, these consequences will manifest and we cannot ignore them pretending not to see them. Our indifference would have caused them whether we cry, "Wolf!" or not.

Indifference is not our ally; it is the ally of the enemy. Evil, in any form it manifests, would progress when we look the other way and say nothing, or when we reduce the problem we are facing to an abstract concept, or when we include it in the list of work and study of a committee that has no power to impose a change. Such a method is a great way for evil to continue its plans and progress. Indifference is one of the favorite ways for evil to spread.

In the darkest times of history, we always had killers and victims, and on a large scale. The worst times were during WWI and WWII. History books talk about the many, many, many millions of people who have been killed. But there were other dark times also, and we don't talk about them – the criminal times of the bystanders.

Bystanders stand near, look, and then look away as if not concerned. They do not participate. They are indifferent to human suffering, and this is what makes them "destroyers." When suffering is reaching millions, and bystanders who have the power to do something do not intervene to change the situation in order to alleviate the suffering, this makes the bystanders mass destroyers. In this context, we seem ready to admit that a nuclear or a biological weapon can cause a mass destruction, but we do not seem ready to admit that indifference can cause a mass destruction too. We prefer not to be in the list of the bystanders.

"Ignore it and it will go away," we usually say. But it doesn't. It will rather grow, expand, and spread. A crime should be confronted and exposed, and not ignored. Turning the blind eye to the corruption in our society and assuming that it is not happening or just ignoring it, is a big problem. Failure to speak out against it and oppose it promotes evil. Unfortunately, apathy, political complacency, and indifference afflict our philosophy of life, lifestyles, and society as a whole. Isn't turning a blind eye to injustice and to a crime accommodated with a complacent silence, worse than, or at least equal to, picking up a gun to fight it?

There is no doubt that in the recent past, and at the present moment, positive things have happened and are still happening – events such as the defeat of Nazism, the collapse of communism, the demise of apartheid, the peace accord in Ireland, the NATO intervention in Kosovo. But why does the world seem indifferent vis-à-vis the minorities of the Middle East or Africa in spite of some timid initiatives to just save face? These minorities certainly appreciate the little help they were offered, but they still need the bigger help – peace. If the world would intervene to stop wars and persecutions, we wouldn't have victims by the millions. Helping to stop the war is by far more efficient than sending tents to the refugees. It is good – very good – to help a victim. But it is better – much better – to provide the right conditions so that we don't have victims in the first place.

Indifference can be a weapon of mass destruction too. It allows humans to be inhuman. Peter Marshall said it well when he said, "A different world cannot be built by indifferent people."

In spiritual life, indifference works in subtle ways like novocaine. One cannot see it, but one can see the consequences of it; it changes our sensitivity towards things. Convictions, values, and priorities are no longer what they once were. We are numb to them. The Commandments become blue laws, devotions no longer mean much, and any spiritual concern vanishes. God is marginalized. God has nothing to do with us anyway. "Who cares!"

Who cares if God exists or not? Do atheists really want God to not exist? Atheists and agnostics are not unanimous on this. Even if they don't want God to directly affect their lives, and even if they consider religion as a system of absurdities and contradictions, some of them still see the practical usefulness the existence of God has for the coherence of society. They think that society would have been worse if God did not exist. Besides that, they do not care. They are indifferent. The only thing that they care about is their pre-occupation with the things of this materialistic world.

Gaudium et Spes (The Pastoral Constitution on the Church in the Modern World of the Second Vatican Council) notes the following:

> Still, many of our contemporaries have never recognized this intimate and vital link with God, or have explicitly rejected it.... Some never get to the point of raising questions about God, since they seem to experience no religious stirrings nor do they see why they should trouble themselves about religion.... Modern civilization itself often complicates the approach to God, not for any essential reason, but because it is excessively engrossed in earthly affairs.... Undeniably, those who willfully shut out God from their hearts and try to dodge religious questions are not following the dictates of their consciences. Hence they are not free of blame. (n. 19)

One can easily detect in these words the phenomenon of religious indifference that is probably the most widespread and the most serious of unbelief. It is neither ignorance nor rejection. It is just disinterestedness and disaffection, and this is what makes it so toxic and a silent killer. In fact, there is no worse patient than the one who does not care about, or pretends to ignore, his or her own illness.

Practically, what we are saying with such an attitude is that we are shifting our love to a finite good that is taking God's place. When we do that, all our priorities and values will shift at the same time. Unavoidably then, different consequences will certainly occur. No wonder the lack of respect for the person, the lack of integrity, the disappearance of family values, and the spread of all forms of violence for a specific reason or for no reason at all would become the new reality – the "new normal." This is mass destruction at different levels, whether we call it this way or not.

No one can deny that the progress and achievements of science and technology in the last two centuries were effective instruments in causing God to disappear ("death of God" – wrong image of God). The techno-scientific achievements have not only fostered prosperity and created the consumer society, but it also brought to human beings a sense of security, maturity, self-sufficiency, and the conviction that we can solve all our problems by ourselves without the necessity of a divine help. Therefore, it is no wonder that we see many of our contemporaries losing interest in inquiring about religion, and they became indifferent to God's presence in their lives; they became deaf and blind to the sublime and the infinite. They lost the sense of wonder and the mystery. Indifference is not indifferent and it cannot be indifferent.

By itself, indifference is a symptom for a deeper disease that is rooted in the very relationship with God and others. When God is not the center and source of spiritual vitality, indifference will be the substitute. We may still go to church and turn to various social and religious remedies to fill the void, but nothing will do if we already lost the very center of a spiritual and human existence. Orthodoxy is good, but it cannot be, by itself, the answer. Orthodoxy is the hearth without the fire. Unless we are enflamed by the Spirit of God, we will remain dry, apathetic, and indifferent. "A different world cannot be built by indifferent people," Peter Marshall reminds us.

9

Our Golden Calves (3)

Idols in Disguise

Since we, generally speaking, believe in God, participate in religious services and church activities, and do everything "right," it won't come to our minds, when we are doing all these "good" things, that it is possible to be idolaters at the same time. This would seem utterly absurd.

Not so fast. We could live a double life, knowingly or unknowingly.

If worshipping idols seems to belong to the ancient world, or to another part of the world and another culture, we should not consider ourselves immune to such a worshipping. The tendency to replace God we do not see, by false gods we see, is the same now as it was a long, long time ago. It is so easy for us to transform God's blessings into idols.

Can we truly and honestly say that we don't have any problem with the First Commandment, "You shall have no other gods before me" (Exodus 20:3)? If we don't keep a golden calf in our garden, this does not mean that we are not worshipping other idols. It may mean that we have very refined idols that we worship in ignorance like the ancient Athenians (see Acts 17:23) and we refuse to admit that we could have been doing so.

The biblical record of Exodus 32, which tells the story of Moses on Mount Sinai and the impatient appeal of the Israelites to Aaron, "Come, make gods for us, who shall go before us; as for this Moses, the man who brought us up out of the land of Egypt, we do not know what has become of him" (Exodus 32:1), is an unmistakable hint on how and why we make gods in today's world as well. The story of the Israelites at the foot of Mount Sinai (see Exodus 32) gives the secret of the basic idolatry formula. Let us go through the ingredients that this chapter describes:

- *Impatience.* "When the people saw that Moses delayed to come down from the mountain, the people gathered around Aaron, and said to him, "Come, make gods for us, who shall go before us; as for this Moses, the man who brought us up out of the land of Egypt, we do not know what has become of him" (Exodus 32:1), Translation: We seem to have an urgent need for instant gratification and the refusal of waiting for God as the Source of our satisfactory answers. Impatient "here and now."

- *Here and now.* "The people gathered around Aaron, and said to him, "Come, make gods for us, who shall go before us" (Exodus 32:1). Translation: We need to see results right here right now. We need a god like us. We create a god like us. We create an idol we relate to, dressed in the clothes of convenience, spontaneity, usefulness, acceptance, and practicality—without waiting "forever."

- *Knowledge.* "This Moses, the man who brought us up out of the land of Egypt, we do not know what has become of him" (Exodus 32:1). Translation: We need to know things and the "why" things happen the way they happen. When we don't have palpable evidence about something, we don't believe in it. Reason, otherwise absurdity. Science, otherwise nonsense. Evidence, otherwise pure fiction. Less faith, more idols.

- *Disdain and ingratitude.* "As for this Moses, the man who brought us up out of the land of Egypt, we do not know what has become of him" (Exodus 32:1). Translation: When we easily forget what God is doing for us and in us as the Israelites forgot that God used Moses as an instrument to save them from slavery, we open wide the door to idolatry. If we neglect the prayer of thanksgiving to our Creator, we become more vulnerable to finding a god of our own making to praise and worship, disdaining—"this Moses," who does he think he is?—and disqualifying any messenger or sign from God.

- *Reversion.* The golden "calf" that the Israelites started to venerate could be considered as a symbol of reversion to what they had in Egypt: the familiar and the comfortable with the known. For them now, it is very uncomfortable to deal with an unknown God who is leading them to an unknown territory. Translation: Spiritual growth can slow down and even stop, if not regress sometimes. Then we are tempted to return to our old ways of being—our most familiar frailties that are a fertile soil for idols.

- *Compromises.* Aaron, according to the story, yielded to the demands of the Israelites to make for them an idol. "He took the gold from them, formed it in a mold, and cast an image of a calf; and they said, 'These are your gods, O Israel, who brought you up out of the land of Egypt!' When Aaron saw this, he built an altar before it; and Aaron made proclamation and said, 'Tomorrow shall be a festival to the Lord'" (Exodus 32:4-5). So everyone is happy. Translation: Often we do not feel the need to reject God when we worship our secret gods. We compromise. We declare allegiance and affection to God and gods, God and culture, God and science, God and denomination, God and anything else. It is God *and*, God *with*, God *alongside*, God *beside*, God *side-by-side with*, God *but also*, God *in addition to*, and the like.

- *Lack of leadership.* "Moses said to Aaron, 'What did this people do to you that you have brought so great a sin upon them?'" (Exodus 32:21). Translation: When leaders stop leading and yield to the weakness and fantasy of those who are supposed to be led, they contribute to the sins of people and bring calamity on them. Then everybody loses while idols flourish.

- *Perversion.* When idols are in place, corruption becomes inevitable. "They rose early the next day, and offered burnt offerings and brought sacrifices of well-being; and the people sat down to eat and drink, and rose up to revel. The Lord said to Moses, 'Go down at once! Your people, whom you brought up out of the land of Egypt, have acted perversely; they have been quick to turn aside from the way that I commanded them; they have cast for themselves un image of a calf, and have worshiped it and sacrificed to it'" (Exodus 32:6-8). Translation: One can present offerings to God and pray and perform all the rituals found in the book, and at the same time indulge in excess and revelry. Corruption is the inescapable outcome of the breaking away from God and worshipping the idols.

Making a god is easy. We've done it, we keep doing it, and we will continue to do it until the day we go back to the First Commandment with our heart and mind—read it, meditate on it, and live by it. Then we will hear, "I am the Alpha and the Omega, the beginning and the end. To the thirsty I will give water as a gift from the spring of the water of life. Those who conquer will inherit these things, and I will be their God and they will be my children" (Revelation 21:6-7). Otherwise, "But as for the cowardly, the faithless, the polluted, the murderers, the fornicators, the sorcerers, the idolaters, and all liars, their place will be in the lake that burns with fire and sulfur, which is the second death" (Revelation 21:8).

These days we may no longer worship statues, but let's not fool ourselves into thinking that we do not worship other forms of "statues." Indeed, we worship our stuff that feeds our desire to acquire as many more things as possible, pulling away our attention from God. We worship our own egos by being obsessed with education, career, self-image building, and social media. We worship humankind by idolizing scientific achievements and believing the illusion that we are the masters of our own destiny. We worship our addictions no matter what they are and no matter what forms they take. We worship our own righteousness by praying like the Pharisee, "God, I thank you that I am not like other people: thieves, rogues, adulterers, or even like this tax collector. I fast twice a week; I give a tenth of all my income" (Luke 18:11), and not needing to repent of anything. The modern-day Pharisee is craving popularity and attention, and taking credit for having won souls to God – the god of self-worshipping at the altar of self-aggrandizement at the expense of others and of God.

The sin of idolatry is more common than we might think, indeed. The following questions are just a few among many that help us discern the hidden and subtle idols – idols in disguise – that run our lives consciously or most likely unconsciously. During a lucid moment of a prayerful reflection, let us ask ourselves:

- In whom, or in what, do we place our trust?
- Deep in our hearts and souls, whom do we expect to guarantee our security and happiness?
- Who, for us, is the source of truth? How can we know if what we think and do is right or wrong?
- Who, or what, can guarantee our future?
- In the most difficult times of our lives, who or what, we think, can take care of us – God, the State, the system, others, or ourselves?

- Do we believe that science can have the answer to everything we ask and that includes the questions of our very existence such as our origins, destiny, and destination?
- To what do our hearts and minds cling?
- What compels us?
- What controls us?
- What drives us?
- What motivates us?
- What rules us?
- What preoccupies our hearts, thoughts, and time?
- What do we crave?
- What is the one thing that we cannot live without?
- What is the thing that, if removed from our life, would cause great pain, despair and depression?
- What is the dream we have that we would sacrifice everything to realize?
- What does our bank statement say our idol is?
- What does the time we spend in doing things say our idol is?
- What does an ideal vacation look like?
- What makes our life meaningful and worth living?
- How much time do we spend with God?

Let us keep in mind that the answer to such questions is not necessarily a "bad" thing in itself. However, we can make of good things, and even "spiritual" things, idols – idols in disguise. For example: a ministry is without question or doubt a very good thing, provided we keep God the central focus. If we shift the central focus to the ministry itself, we would create an idol; God is the goal not the religious practice itself. We can say the same thing about our strengths, gifts, and achievements and accomplishments. We can say also the same thing when we move to a new place, find a new job, develop a new relationship, work for a new cause, or enter into a new circumstance. When these things become more important than God, they become the idols in disguise.

Anything – good or bad – has the potential to become an idol when we allow it to rule us, compel us, and control us. Then what we are saying is that this or that idol is my new god, for "No one can serve two masters" (Matthew 6:24).

"Spiritual but Not Religious"

It has recently become quite common and, in some circles, fashionable and even imperative to distinguish between spirituality and religion -- spirituality as exalted with everything positive and religion as saddled with everything negative. No wonder we very often hear the popular "I am spiritual but not religious" or just SBNR.

Such a distinction between what is spiritual and what is religious is relatively new; throughout the ages these two words have been used interchangeably by scholars of theology, philosophy, sociology, and psychology. Even though the 19th century started to see a separation between spirituality and religion, their disconnection did not occur before the end of the Second World War. Then spirituality became more oriented on subjective experience especially at the influence of humanistic psychology, mystical and esoteric traditions, eastern religions, secularism, the worldly mentality – individualist, consumerist, hedonist, etc. – and later the advent of the New Age movement and the concern for being "spiritually correct."

Although, in the past, there was no clear cut between what was spiritual and what was religion, our culture, at the present time, wants us to believe there is a clear one, and that is because of the way it defines spirituality and religion.

What do Spirituality and religion mean today?

Let us consider a few definitions drawn from the Internet (http://nccc.georgetown.edu/body_mind_spirit/definitions_spirituality_religion.html):

Spirituality:

1. "the experience or expression of the sacred" (Adapted from Random House Dictionary of the English Language, 1967).

2. "...the search for transcendent meaning" – can be expressed in religious practice or ...expressed "exclusively in their relationship to nature, music, the arts, a set of philosophical beliefs, or relationships with friends and family" (Astrow et al. 2001).

3. "individual search for meaning" (Bown and Williams 1993).

4. "the search for meaning in life events and a yearning for connectedness to the universe" (Coles 1990).

5. "a person's experience of, or a belief in, a power apart from his or her own existence" (Mohr 2006).

6. "a quality that goes beyond religious affiliation, that strives for inspiration, reverence, awe, meaning and purpose, even in those who do not believe in God. The spiritual dimension tries to be in harmony with the universe, strives for answers about the infinite, and comes essentially into focus in times of emotional stress, physical (and mental) illness, loss, bereavement and death" (Murray and Zentner 1989:259).

7. ...refers to a broad set of principles that transcend all religions. Spirituality is about the relationship between ourselves and something larger. That something can be the good of the community or the people who are served by your agency or school or with energies greater than ourselves. Spirituality means being in the right relationship with all that is. It is a stance of harmlessness toward all living beings and

an understanding of their mutual interdependence." (Kaiser 2000)

Religion:

1. "a set of beliefs and practices related to the issue of what exists beyond the visible world, generally including the idea of the existence of a being, group of beings, an external principle or a transcendent spiritual entity" (Adapted from Random House Dictionary of the English Language, 1967).

2. "set of beliefs, practices, and language that characterizes a community that is searching for transcendent meaning in a particular way, generally based upon belief in a deity" (Astrow et al. 2001).

3. religious beliefs – "formed within the context of practices and rituals shared by a group to provide a framework for connectedness to God" (Davies, Brenner, Orloff, Sumner, and Worden 2002).

4. "an organized system of practices and beliefs in which people engage … a platform for the expression of spirituality…" (Mohr 2006).

5. "outward practice of a spiritual system of beliefs, values, codes of conduct, and rituals" (Speck 1998).

These definitions seem to be close to each other and different at the same time, compatible and incompatible, clear and ambiguous. They almost spell that everything bad lies with religion while everything good can be found in spirituality. Religion is about control and it does not necessarily lead a person to the sacred and to God. Spirituality is the way to the sacred and to God.

In reality, spirituality and religion are not contradictory ideas, and do not and should not exclude each other. They complement each other, in the search for inner peace, for world peace, and for a fulfilled and purposeful life. The best would be when religion is spiritual and spirituality is religious.

What does spirituality mean after all?

Spirituality is a nebulous term, as it means different things to different people. For some people, it means being concerned with the practice of a religion and their union with God. For others, it refers to the life of the spirit and has nothing to do with what we normally experience in everyday life.

Some see spirituality in the adherence to a set of strict rules and dogmas. Others believe that they are spiritual when they have a devotional attitude toward a charismatic leader or when they belong to a religious community of any kind.

The truth of the matter is that spirituality does not mean being just "spiritual." Our spiritual life is supposed to embrace our life in all its daily aspects—physical, emotional, intellectual, psychological, economic, social, religious, and any others. Nothing should be taken away, nor thrown into the trash dump. Whatever we are should belong.

If we don't find God in the concrete, the particular, and the ordinary, we are not going to find God in the extraordinary and the esoteric either.

Without going into complicated definitions, we can perhaps spell out some characteristics that describe best that what we call "spirituality."

First, spirituality is concerned with the way we treat others and the way we deal with our circumstances in life. Our own feelings or opinions about someone or about a special event are not enough. We must put ourselves into the walking shoes of that person who bothers us or likes us, and look deeply into what is happening, and see what ongoing events mean.

Second, spirituality is concerned with all of our potentials and how we employ them in our daily practical life.

Third, spirituality is concerned with the deeper meanings behind things, as they appear to be. It is interested in their causes and purposes. By understanding this basic truth, one can become like the light that illuminates all things around. Here clarity is a key word: clarity in the things seen, and clarity in the one who sees them.

Fourth, spirituality, in the Christian sense, has the Christ dimension within it. It sees Christ in all things and all things in Christ. It is the Holy Spirit in action. It is Christian life as it is supposed to be—totally and not fragmented on this or that aspect of life.

In this sense, a more integrated and holistic understanding of the human person is urgently sought and lived. What was yesteryear materialistic, negative, and secular is, because of the mystery of the Incarnation, no longer necessarily so. With the Incarnation, the "civil" war within us between what is spiritual and what is material should have been already ended. Indeed, matter, the human body included, is God-made and it is holy. Artists no longer have to necessarily choose between sacred or secular subjects. Each experience of beauty is an experience of God. Our relationship to God is no longer only vertical as if God is "up there" and we are "down here." No. Our relationship to God is also horizontal, for God is all in all. Christ is in all things and all things are in Christ. This is the depth of spiritual life: a feeling of sacredness of all things as all things are in Christ, and a feeling of holiness as Christ is in all things.

All of life, then, becomes a central part of the divine mystery, and what we used to call profane, as opposed to sacred, is vanishing little by little from our vocabulary. Only the sacred remains and encompasses everything. Holiness is not a denial, but an affirmation—the most positive affirmation there is.

What is the difference between spirituality and religion?

Spirituality and religion are so close that many people talk about the one when they mean the other. However, there are differences and nuances between the two. In fact, one can be religious without being spiritual, and be spiritual without necessarily being religious.

The religious traditions usually divide the world into the sacred and the profane. Holy lands, temples, churches, Lourdes, Jerusalem, Mecca, and so many other places are thought to have special interests for all the visiting believers. When believers go to those places, they expect to experience a special touch from the divine. The spiritual quest does not have special places that are sacred, as every place is sacred and no place is profane. A beautiful lake, a majestic mountain, and the Grand Canyon can be sanctuaries. They can be, in a spiritual person's eye, as sacred as the holy places just mentioned.

Religion as such—not as life in Christ—is a belief system, a set of dogmas, and a well-organized and structured community that reports to a prophet, a teacher, or a charismatic figure of leadership. Spirituality is the ability to discover our inner self and unique special-ness, and use these qualities in the way we think is right. Religion does not allow us this freedom. Spirituality does; it allows us to be positive and creative in a broader sense. A spiritual person may or may not use the rules practiced in a religion as tools to reach a goal.

At the beginning of religion, there is a known God and revelation. At the beginning of the spiritual quest, there is an unknown God and there are the questions of the seeker.

Religion asserts that humans are imperfect and sinful and in need of religion to set them straight and guide them how to improve themselves. Spirituality asserts that the person is inherently perfect, whole, and lovable; spirituality will help, then, to realize this truth. Religion does have rules about the seeking. Spirituality has guidelines but not rules. Religion may put an intermediary between the individual and God (a pastor, for example). Spirituality invites the individual to talk to God directly and hear the divine response. Religion may be seen as a container for spirituality while spirituality would like to see the individual himself or herself as a container for divine energy.

In religion there is usually a more or less clear map that the faithful are expected to respect and follow on their journeys. In the spiritual quest, life is an uncharted adventure in which one does not take orders on the journey from anyone, and whose chief quality would be the amazing openness to what may come next.

Religion is usually a formal institution and corporate. Spirituality can be individual or communal, but with very loose structures.

In religion, we count heavily on rituals and on the one who is behind them and whom we seek to please, for healing the self and others. In spirituality, we count rather on the self, as if the self is the real source that generates the healing process.

Religion is often about loyalty to institutions, clergy, rituals, and rules. Spirituality is more about loyalty to meaningfulness, justice, compassion, and peace. Religion is often time forced on the individual while spirituality is rather chosen. Religion has a certain number of dogmas one is supposed to believe. Spirituality counts on reason that invites to personal decisions with their consequences. Religion speaks of sin and guilt. Spirituality invites us to learn from errors without feeling remorse for which has already passed. Religion may become a cause for division and conflict. Spirituality may become a reason for union and reconciliation. Religion is more about the "to do." Spirituality is more about the "to be." Religion makes one think of the after-life life and of paradise. Spirituality makes one focus on living life here and now. Religion believes in the past, the future, and eternal life. Spirituality believes in living in the present moment and in the consciousness of all that is. Religion insists on the one true. Spirituality insists on the all true. Both religion and spirituality are looking for the truth and the communion with the divine. But both are mistaken when religious people worship institutions and regulations instead of God, and when spiritual people take their idea of God for the actual God but now defined in a way to suit themselves. Both are mistaken when religion uses its dogmas, as some people believe, to control others, control political power, and control property and wealth, and when spirituality claims ownership of awakening as a the result of the sole practice of mindfulness, meditation , and personal reflection.

Religion indicates the way of salvation. Spirituality allows the individual to achieve the goal of full awakening by whatever path is right for him or her. Religion seems to say, "Ask God for power and you become truly free." Spirituality seems to say, "Be strong; you can do it."

Most of us are born affiliated by a geographical destiny and social condition for being what we are. We are born Christians, Muslims, Buddhists, Jews, or belong to another affiliation, or sometimes without religion at all. Unless there is intervention on our part for a change, this is usually what determines our identity, our values, and the way we think and see the world; our "identity" defines us more than we define our identity. No wonder spirituality seems more extensive than any one religion in particular. Does this mean that we should be spiritual and not religious? Not necessarily. The best path is to be both religious and spiritual at the same time. Spirituality, alone, has many problems and pitfalls.

What are the problems and pitfalls of spirituality?

Considered alone, without being accompanied by religious convictions and secure structures, spirituality has its own risks. Here are some of its problems and pitfalls.

a. *The flight inward.* Even though spirituality, as we understand it today with its holistic approach, has a global view of the person, the reality remains that the emphasis goes to the life of the soul, the inner life. If the Bible and traditions no longer present a sense of belonging and security, the pitfall would be to go farther and farther in the inner world of the soul and stay in the shaky ground of mere subjectivity.

b. *Self-preoccupation.* "My prayer life," My spiritual life," My spiritual journey," are some of the phrases we hear every day when we talk about spirituality. Sometimes our self-preoccupation is so exaggerated that it tends to eclipse others' lives, almost totally. We know that any meaningful spirituality must be always open to others. Spiritual life is not a solitary path, but a multifaceted journey of companions. Spirituality should never be divorced from the wisdom of a community.

c. *Self-therapy*. It seems that the therapeutic aspect of life is more and more associated with spirituality rather than with religion. Without doubt, affirmation and visualization play a big role in the psychology of the individual. But, they are not everything. There is no substitute whatsoever for the grace of God for healing our own wounded-ness, brokenness, and sickness.

d. *Proliferation of spiritualities*. To have too many kinds of spiritualities, per se, is not a bad thing. It shows the richness of the soul and the great adaptability of the human being. So we can have different schools or types of spirituality such as: Trinitarian spirituality, Benedictine spirituality, Augustinian spirituality, Franciscan spirituality, Thomistic spirituality, Ignatian spirituality, Teresian spirituality, or spirituality of the Desert Fathers and Mothers, and the French school, and so on. There is also the spirituality of single people, of the married, of the separated, of the divorced. There is spirituality for the ministry, for the sisterhood, for the brotherhood, the priesthood, and for the laity. There is a spirituality of childhood, the middle-aged, and the aging. Also, there is African-American spirituality, Hispanic spirituality, American spirituality, other ethnic groups and countries' spirituality, feminist spirituality, and male spirituality. There is holistic spirituality, bio-ecological spirituality, and global spirituality. There is incarnational spirituality, vital spirituality, existential spirituality, negative spirituality, positive spirituality, cataphatic spirituality, and apophatic spirituality. Also, there is spirituality of the Cross, spirituality of the ideal, and spirituality of the real, and so on.

Although this proliferation of spiritualities have many advantages, they may however lead us into lack of clarity and confusion, and to lack of clarity, especially when some of them seem to contradict each other instead of complementing each other.

Steps toward a better understanding of spirituality

I would like to join my voice to the many other voices and predict that this millennium, in spite of all appearances, is going to be a spiritual millennium. At the present time, we are in a unique historical period, one that no other age before us has experienced. While some of us are looking deeply into the past for inspiration, others are concerned with, and motivated by, the future of life and the life of the future. And everyone, somehow, is thirsty for the divine and the real meaning of life.

Since the Internet and all other media of communication are becoming available to almost everyone, information and experiences are now widely shared. We feel compelled to find a new way of living, based on seeing the holy within the profane.

The vision of the sacred, hidden in the secular, is not an appeal to abandon prayer, worship, pilgrimages, and other traditional devotions. Beside continuing to do the same things as before, we now experience the sacred in the commonplaces of everyday life. I would like to call this spirituality "spirituality of integration" or simply "spirituality of the ordinary." This is a real challenge, for we know how difficult it is to change our attitudes and belief systems. It is also a challenging reality, for this is perhaps the most effective way to reach our inner and outer peace, both at a personal level and at the level of the entire world.

To operate effectively, such spirituality has certain basic tenets, with emphasis particularly on the *Incarnation*, *God's activity in the world*, *love*, *globalization*, *new asceticism*, and *fullness of life*.

The *Incarnation* has profoundly touched our very nature and affected the very roots of our consciousness. With God having taken a human body, being able to be seen, touched, held, and listened to, something totally different, never experienced before, happened. God took a human face, became accessible, available, and vulnerable, and chose relationships as the best way to be understood. Jesus, by revealing the true nature of a loving God to us, and the necessity of loving one another, created the most solid bond known to humanity. He entered "matter" to be the element of completion, fulfillment, and hence redemption of all created reality. Even though the Incarnation occurred at a specific time and place, the truth is that this Incarnation, as well as the act of Creation and the Redemption, must be considered a continuing process. Christ means God at work in the world. With the Word becoming flesh, everyone and everything has become mystically flesh and body of the Word. No one and nothing is left behind in this new reality of an integrated universe.

Christianity is the only religion that has the mystery of the Incarnation. It is the only religion based on God-made-human-being and salvation through the Redemption. The Incarnation should have ended the tensions and adversity between spirit and matter, body and soul, and spiritual life and ordinary human life. God's approach was not adversity, but integration and harmony. Why do we live sometimes as though the Incarnation never happened? Our Christian spirituality must be grounded in the continuous process of the Creation-Incarnation-Redemption mystery. The Holy Spirit brings all things together into full wholeness. In spiritual life, nothing should be taken away. Everything should be integrated. Spirituality is real, for reality is spiritual. A spirituality that rejects what is of human reality is not a true Christian spirituality. The spirituality of the ordinary must be our ordinary spirituality.

God is an *active agent* in human history. Being created in the image of God means, among other things, that God has given us the potential of limitless growth so that we would increasingly be able to manifest, within and through us, the divine infinity. The image of God here is not a static state; it is rather a dynamic way of becoming more and more the living Christ. The early Fathers of the Church did not hesitate to talk about deification. This is indeed what it is. Everyone can write the biography of the Holy Spirit in his or her life, "for it is God who is at work in you" (Philippians 2:13). When we allow the Holy Spirit to work freely in us and in the world through us, we give this Spirit birth, again and again, in the world. Our interaction with the Holy Spirit's activity is called the flame of love.

Love is the energy that brings everything together—from the smallest to the biggest. Love is the dynamic energy of evolution and transformation, at the personal level as well as at the social level. Nothing can be changed for the better except through love. The flame of love has the most powerful force to unite, to transform, to make whole, to heal, to create, to feel God's presence, to be one with God—to become "god." Love, therefore, is not simply a code of perfection; it is the fundamental dynamism of the very act of creation, and the continuous process of transformation. If we do not love, we cannot fully exist. More love leads to more consciousness. More consciousness entails more growth in our spirituality and more zest for living to the fullest. Isn't this what Christian life is all about, after all? God is nothing but total and perfect love manifested in the Creation, Incarnation, and Redemption. "Everyone who loves is born of God and knows God" (1 John 4:7).

Globalization. Love is not about the "what about me?" concern. In its essence, love is open to more ground with fewer and fewer boundaries. This is why we talk today of interrelationship, interconnectedness, interdependence, globalization, holistic approaches to this or that, and about the civilization of the universal. No wonder the word "global" appears so often and will appear more and more as time goes by. We talk, for example, about global communications, global economy, global network, global trends, global business, global marketing, global consciousness, global concerns, global education, global spirituality.... Yes, yes, yes. We absolutely need a global spirituality above all other kinds of globalism. It is the responsibility of spiritual people to awaken others and to prepare them for this third millennium, which should be the millennium of integration of all human beings together, along with nature, the entire cosmos, and God. Shouldn't we take another look—in a more comprehensive way this time—at the theology of the Mystical Body of Christ?

New asceticism. With the Word becoming flesh, all things were supposed to change. "So, if anyone is in Christ," wrote Saint Paul, "there is a new creation: everything old has passed away; see, everything has become new!" (2 Corinthians 5:17) Everything has become new in Jesus Christ. It is very important to realize—even though many of us still live as if the Incarnation has not yet happened—that a new approach for unity has been established between spirit and matter, soul and body, and divine and human. We have become whole by the power of the Holy Spirit. This should mean that the conflict that existed between spirit and matter should have been over by now. When we understand this, we start to engage ourselves in new forms of asceticism that are not less, but much more, demanding. Indeed, being positive in life is much more demanding than being negative. Pondering reality as it is, which is the ground for our spiritual life, is more demanding than just denying it, or fearing it, and withdrawing into a hermitage. Being involved in world affairs and helping solve problems caused by new situations is more difficult than just ignoring them and pretending that they do not exist. Finding God precisely where we are is more demanding than finding God at the Sunday church service. Being generous in giving time to serving others is more demanding than being generous in giving money to the poor, especially when the money we give is a surplus or an amount that helps to reduce taxes. Being really loving, caring, and sensitive to others is more demanding than carrying out a simple—and, sometimes, "detached"—duty to others. Being joyful with others is more demanding than feeling pity for their misfortunes. Being a responsible, loving, and very concerned spouse, especially in today's world, is more demanding than living in a place that is protected by walls, rules, and the wrong interpretation of the necessity of fleeing the world. Working in changing the structures that let people remain poor and sick, or be killed, is more demanding than making eloquent speeches on justice and health care, or expressing "deep" sorrow in the two-hour ceremony for victims. Matching one's life with one's preaching is more demanding than one's unmatched "should and ought to" litanies. Not compromising in the values of the gospel is more demanding than just scoring "good deeds" for eternal life.

Fullness of life. To be more spiritual is to be more human. Christian spirituality should build upon, and perfect, the humanity in each person, rather than neglect it, deny it, or even destroy it. When we see Christ in all things, we recognize the divine element working in, and transforming, all things. Therefore, everything must grow into greater fullness of being. With Christ at the center of everything, we affirm the fullness of life. True Christian life and true human life are not two different lives. Together, they form a new reality—the fullness of life.

Then there is no need to choose between being either religious or spiritual. We are both/and – religious and spiritual.

A Conservative God vs. a Liberal God

Is God conservative or liberal? The answer depends on who we are rather than on God . God does not use labels. We do. "Conservative," "liberal," "right wing," "left wing," "traditionalist," "progressive," "fundamentalist," "moderate" are human inventions. Perception remains the key for explaining things. We seem to have been creating reality in our own image for a long time, and we are very good at it. God is part of that reality we are creating and we want to see that "creation" on our side.

When a candidate who is running for office says, for example, "God is on my side – a vote for me is a vote for God," what does this tell you? When another candidate, who is concerned with the perfect "photo op," visits Sunday church services, singing hymns, shaking hands with ministers and parishioners, and saying the "right" words in regard to family values and social issues while having himself or herself different convictions, what does this tell you? President Abraham Lincoln responded famously to this kind of questions by saying: "Sir, my concern is not whether God is on our side; my greatest concern is to be on God's side, for God is always right."

But no, we see God on the side of the way we see our social issues. We operate out of certain hidden, or not so hidden, software (ideology, philosophy, anthropology, ecclesiology, hermeneutical-filter, political agenda…) as if we were unable to see reality as it is. Our perception runs always on labels and biases.

What do conservative ideologies say on the subject?

Generally speaking (not all the conservatives are really conservative), "conservatives" want to "conserve" and preserve established traditions and human values, with a particular emphasis on individual rights and responsibilities. While advocating for a small government, they want to see its role more or less restricted to restraining evil, protecting citizens, and providing laws and moral codes that serve as a foundation for society. They also believe that individuals must be free to make their own decisions and accept the consequences of these decisions. Consequently, it seems to them that it does not matter, except for a few days, if one individual invades a school and opens fire on a multitude of students and teachers, because that individual has the right to posses arms according to the constitution, and no one has the right to deny this right, even if these arms were used not in self-defense but with the clear intention to kill others..

Conservatives disagree in general with government programs that tend to redistribute wealth to aid the poor, to favor tax cuts in the name of economic growth, and to dispute laws regulating narcotics or abortion. Also, they distrust international institutions like the UN, for example, and support aggressive foreign policy that helps in spreading democracy.

Conservatives tend to believe in, and rely on, the infinite wisdom of God who already defines for us what is right and what is wrong. They can say "yes" to prayer in public schools; display the Ten Commandments at government facilities; limit the legal definition of marriage to "one man, one woman"; be advocates for traditional family values and the rejection of abortion. If, "My greatest concern is to be on God's side, for God is always right," as Lincoln said, this concretely means that God takes side on certain issues, that certain people will be divinely "justified," and that certain others will not be "justified" because they stand in opposition.

Pushed to the extreme, and because of its theocratic foundation, conservatism, as some people argue, caused the holy wars, jihads, terrorism, and paradoxically, radical atheism in reaction.

The truth then is found in what fits this way of thinking, as if a conservative is always right.

What do liberal ideologies say on the subject?

Generally speaking (not all the liberals are really liberal), "liberals" put emphasis on community and equality concepts. For them, since individuals will not necessarily act in ways that serve the common good, government therefore is necessary to regulate affairs and promote equality and justice. They usually favor progress and reform in political and religious affairs. They trust the power of ideas to produce change.

Liberals believe that, without the government help, the structural and institutional problems in society will hardly have a solution. Therefore, liberals find themselves supporting government policies and programs in regard to the essential needs such as education, health care, housing, civil rights, workers rights, and the environment.

Liberals tend not to believe in, and rely on, the infinite wisdom of God. Instead, they would like to believe in, and rely on, the human wisdom. Therefore, they find themselves more inclined to determine what is right and what is wrong according to what the culture of the day says it is. A liberal woman has the right to do whatever she pleases with her body. A liberal man can love whoever he wishes, whenever he wishes, the way he wishes, and as long as he wishes. A liberal court can ban displaying the Ten Commandments in public buildings. A liberal school can ban prayer and religious studies in the name of freedom of conscience. A liberal parent can tolerate a disobedient child in the name of the respect and the right to one's own opinion. Here, abortion is called "being responsible." Here, "safe sex" is more practical than abstinence. Here, denying same-sex couples the right to marry is viewed as intolerant and judgmental.

Liberals advocate concepts of maximum individual freedom and want the government to protect civil liberties.

The truth then is found in what fits this way of thinking, as if a liberal is always right.

Is God conservative?

Of course God is conservative – and by far more conservative than the most intolerant conservative there is or there was.

Please, just take a deep breath and calm down. God is conservative but not a right winged invader or an abortion clinic bomber.

Since the beginning, God told Adam and Eve what they can do and what they cannot do (see Genesis 3) then, God revealed the Ten Commandments (see Exodus 20:1-17) and stated that there is a right behavior and there is a wrong behavior. God also explained the penalties when one does the wrong thing and breaks the laws (see Leviticus 26:14-39). God will bring the furious wrath upon those who disobey Him (see Nahum 1-2), destruction on the wicked (see Psalms 37:20), and God will "by no means [clear] the guilty" (Exodus 34:7). Also, God gave humankind dominion over the earth and over the animals (see Genesis 1:26-30) and enabled him to get wealth (see Deuteronomy 8:18). God also, one can argue, agreed with small government, low taxes, and strong military (see Isaiah 9:6; 37:36; Hebrews 12:22).

Can any conservative match such conservatism?

Is God liberal?

Of course God is liberal – and by far more liberal than the most tolerant liberal there is or there was.

Please, just take another deep breath and calm down. God is liberal but not a left-winged relativist whose only principle is not to have one. Even though the word "liberal" does not sound like a highly esteemed word, God is more liberal than one thinks.

God is merciful and gracious (see Psalms 116:5). God promised to bless and care (see Deuteronomy 28:1-14). God loves all human beings (see John 3:16), and promised that one day all nations will be blessed (see Genesis 26:4) doing away with all pain, sorrow and death (see Revelation 21:4).

God is the first to believe in social programs such as supporting the widows and the homeless, taking care of the orphans and the poor, receiving the strangers and the lonely, and visiting the sick and the prisoners.

God believes in the redistribution of wealth (see Proverbs 13:22; 19:17; Exodus 12:35-36) by making sure not to oppress the impoverished by exacting interest from them (Exodus 22:25), granting a remission of debts by a fair and forgiving standard (see Deuteronomy 15:1-2), and making sure all their needs are met (see Deuteronomy 15:7-11). God also requires farmers to leave enough crops during the harvest season "for the alien, the orphan, and the widow" (Deuteronomy 24:19-22). Also, God gave the responsibility for humankind to take care of the earth (see Genesis 2:15); Leviticus 25:1-4). This means that humankind has the power to use the earth but not to abuse it.

"God is love" (1 John 4:8). This is what the definition of God is.

Can any liberal match such liberalism?

God Is God

God is beyond left and right and beyond all labels. But we cannot see God except through our own lenses and biases. Therefore, we usually end up creating God in our own image and in the way we prefer God to be. In this sense, a deformed god is created every day.

God perfectly combines swift justice and infinite compassion. In God's kingdom, it is both/and, and not either/or. This is God's policy and how the kingdom of God looks like. This is also what real love is. The rest is a continuous struggle of human interpretation or misinterpretation.

Only the truth can set us free, no matter what the "color" of our speech. On the Day of Judgment, we will hear: well done, good and faithful child, you have followed the Ten Commandments and did all your religious duties, and you also spent more time concerned about your neighbors in need, fighting global epidemics, protecting the sanctity of life, and finding ways to reach world peace.

One day, a lawyer asked Jesus a question to test him.

"Teacher, which commandment in the law is the greatest?" He said to him, 'You shall love the Lord your God with all your heart, and with all your soul, and with all your mind.' This is the greatest and first commandment. And a second is like it: 'You shall love your neighbor as yourself.' On these two commandments hang all the law and the prophets. (Matthew 22:36-40)

St. Augustine summarized well the way we are supposed to live. He said: "In essentials, unity; in non-essentials, liberty; in all things, charity." This is exactly what God is – love.

Could God be a drug?

Is religion "the opium of the people," as Karl Marx stated? Can religion be "comparable to a childhood neurosis" or "an illusion and it derives its strength from the fact that it falls in with our instinctual desires," as Sigmund Freud imagined? Could God be a drug similar to spiritual marijuana? Is it conceivable that God can be used as a drug, and possibly be even more efficient than any other drug?

Is God a drug?

In the way some people practice their religion, it seems obvious that God is reduced to a simple drug that helps to fix things by ways of religiosity. Religiosity, then, becomes another addiction like alcoholism, for example, or smoking, or gambling, or any other addiction.

Religious addicts want God to take away any problems they may have without taking responsibility for anything themselves. They just go and perform the rituals as perfectly as possible in the hope that these rituals will magically transform undesirable circumstances into desirable ones. Such an attitude is not different from the attitude of someone who puts a quarter or two in the vending machine, and pushes the appropriate button, and *voilà*, he or she has the desired piece of chocolate, or the little bag of potato chips, or the preferred bottle of soda. Of course God fixes things and provides what one needs. But God does not operate as a "fixer" or as a vending machine.

Some other people seem to reduce religion, and particularly their concept of God, to a strong feeling like a kind of "spiritual marijuana." All that they care about is the spiritual high – a deep feeling of ecstasy. Indeed, it is great to be high on God and with all that is related to the divine. Who doesn't like a warm, comfortable, content and homelike feeling of well being with God? However, the truth is that this was the feeling that one enjoyed yesterday, and not necessarily today.

What has happened today? It seems like God has deserted the "happy high" too soon. Where is God in our here and now daily life? What has changed? Circumstances have changed but not God who was and still is the same yesterday, today, and forever (see Hebrews 13:8).

Life is not only a series of beautiful vistas' mountaintop feelings. Life can also lead us into deep dark canyons and valleys of shadow experiences. The banquet of emotional warmth and spiritual well being of one day can be, and usually is, followed by dry days of frustration, incomprehension, and dark nights of the heart and the soul. That is life, and the "God-drug" cannot do much about it except to provide a temporary "high."

A joyful spiritual "high" like this keeps members of the same faith coming back for more. This phenomenon is noticed in the big celebration of any religion. Often it is obvious during the Vatican celebrations, for example, and even more so in the mega-churches' services and the charismatic movements' euphoria. Big crowds' exaltation has been shown to change brain chemistry and to play an important role in social interactions. Since such an atmosphere appeals to emotions and shared experiences, it is no wonder if one hears someone say, for example: "God's love becomes... such a drug that you can't wait to come and get your next hit. ... You can't wait to get involved to get the high from God." One can also hear: "You can look up to the balcony and see the Holy Spirit go over the crowd like a wave in a football game." What makes things more attractive and emotionally more contagious for the people who attend these services is the use of state-of-the-art technology in addition to the comforting messages delivered usually by very talented leaders who feature services in a come-as-you-are atmosphere.

Furthermore, it would be legitimate in this context to ask: Why in the world are people ready to kill other people for God's sake? Why do young people from the West leave everything behind to join a war that is not theirs? What is the real driving force – a principle, a cause, an act of rejection of the status quo, a weapon seduction, a fascination with the idea of a martyr death, magical new sensations, a Freudian religion illusion, a God-drug – that makes people so different, so unusual, so incomprehensible? What is it?

Even though we may not know for sure the real answers to such questions, we certainly know the symptoms of a "God-drug spirituality" that are not very difficult to detect. Here are some of them:

1. *A compulsive and scrupulous concern for spiritual exercises.* Not only there is nothing wrong with prayer, going to church, retreat, quoting scriptures, etc., but they are all recommended. However, when we force our beliefs and practices on others to the point of becoming angry, hostile, and even violent if they choose not to accept all our ways of thinking and living our religion, our religiosity becomes abusive. The reality is that when we shut ourselves away from others, we shut ourselves away from God that we pretend to be close to and to serve.

2. *A judgmental and intolerant attitude.* Because they very often feel chosen and claim to have received special messages from God, religious addicts tend to have a profoundly judgmental and intolerant attitude toward

anyone who does not think the way they think. They can even be violent, verbally or physically, toward everyone who is wrong; everyone is wrong if he or she does not think their way.

3. *A simplistic black and white approach to life.* At the human condition level, only a few situations in life are crystal clear, for most of them are not. Are we sure of our certainties? Do we see life in terms of right and wrong, good and bad, saved and sinner, "us" and "them"? Do we have the tendency to disqualify anyone who does not think the way we think, and reject anything that does not fit into our frame of reference? The "God-drug" spirituality will never tolerate another opinion. Consequently, wars are bound to happen.

4. *A complete denial of personal responsibility while relying solely on the magical divine intervention for having things fixed.* Everyone has problems. How we deal with these problems is the major concern. One can face these problems and try to find solutions. Another can deny their existence. Still another can put the blame on someone else. The "God-drug" addicts will just sit and wait for God to do things for them. They believe that God will magically fix anything.

5. *An obsessive adherence to rules, codes, guidelines, scripts, and instructions.* Where does an intense need to follow rules and rituals come from? One answer could be found in the desire of being more perfect. Another answer could be the fear of punishment if one violates guidelines and instructions. Another answer could be that only the "good old time" with its authenticity has the only and right solution for the present and the future. Still another answer could be that one could use laws and codes in order to have more authority and control. Furthermore, and this is the "God-drug" answer and the worst of all, is when one makes

a god of the rules and the rituals. God cannot be just rules and rituals.

6. *A devaluation of the importance of science and medicine.* Science and religion should work together in the search for truth. They are meant to reach the same truth from different angles. Religious addicts see conflicts between the two. For them, it is better to leave everything to God and decline any other responsibility. Therefore, science, medicine, education, psychology, anthropology, sociology, or any other discipline are good when they conform to their beliefs, and are doubtful and even unacceptable if they present a different point of view. They have a real fear of anything different.

7. *An inability to think and act freely.* Unable to evaluate for themselves the validity and appropriateness of an idea or situation without referring to their mental codes, religious addicts find themselves isolated in their narrow views of the world. They are, in reality, sending back to God one of God's greatest gifts to humankind: freedom. For them, freedom is dangerous and difficult; too much responsibility.

8. *A life living in an imaginary and constructed world instead of the real and concrete world.* Religious addicts usually construct their own universe. What is real for them is what they believe, and not what is out there in the world.

God has created us as co-creators. In the image and likeness of God we were created. What did we do with this precious gift?

We created the concept of God in our own image – the way we are and the way we think. We created traditions, laws, and rules. We created barriers, walls, and divisions. We created churches, schisms, and denominations. We created religions, doctrines, and ways of salvation. We created theories, arguments, and belief systems. We created conflicts, clashes, and wars. We created self-interest, self-satisfaction, self-sufficiency, and self-independence.

This is not what God had in mind when we were created in the image of God. God is love and we were supposed to mirror this love. Instead, we tend to prefer not to deal with the true definition of God or, if this is more convenient, we become religious addicts. Let us conclude this chapter with the explanation that Father Leo Booth has provided in his book, *When God Becomes a Drug: Breaking the Chains of Religious Addiction & Abuse* (Los Angeles, CA: Jeremy P. Tarcher, Inc., 1991, 38):

> I define religious addiction as using God, a church, or a belief system as an escape from reality, in an attempt to find or elevate a sense of self-worth or well-being. It is using God or religion as a fix. It is the ultimate form of codependency – feeling worthless in and of ourselves and looking outside ourselves for something or someone to tell us we are worthwhile. Thus it is an unhealthy relationship with God. It is using God, religion, or a belief system as a weapon against ourselves or others.

Dearest Google, "Who Is My God?"

Like it or not, our unstoppable technology revolution is changing by the day and maybe by the hour. At the same time, it is changing our world.

Now, in a matter of seconds, and at anytime – day and night – we have the capacity to know what is going on at the furthest corner of the earth. Plus, we can reach anyone anywhere, and anyone can also reach us from anywhere at any time.

What a liberation! What a tyranny!

Technology has become the close friend of transparency and of availability, and the bitter enemy of privacy and reverence.

Are we more human this way, or less human? Did our computerized world add another solid stone to the edifice of human civilization or did it contribute to its decline and eventual destruction?

Of course, social media can be incredibly rewarding, helping us know everything we need to know, connect with every one we need to connect with, and exchange opinions with anyone who would like to exchange opinions. In this sense, virtual community can become a real community if we choose to make it real.

We used to be in the community that was defined by our family, neighbors, friends, or the group we belonged to. Now, with our smart-phones and other electronic devices, we can be in touch with our chosen "personal community" or "online community." We can be in touch with a list of people as long as we wish it to be, no matter where they happen to be, near or far, and no matter what ethnic group they belong to or what language they speak. Now, inventors are also talking about smart watches. Soon, another smart-"something else" will certainly emerge. Please notice that, when they introduce the new devices in the market, the word "personal" is often mentioned. But how personal do we want to get?

Do we really need to have our television on, day and night, take our phones with us to bed, and feel the necessity to take a picture when we simply eat a meal or meet someone we don't know yet or even someone we already know? Why do we feel somewhat guilty if we don't stay up-to-date on the twenty-four-hour nonstop feed out of the twenty-four-hour society we have become? Our machines and equipments are designed to run continuously without concerns, neither for day or night nor for here or there. Connections, decisions, deals, and opportunities occur unceasingly, because there is always daytime somewhere and there is always someone ready to talk and make a deal.

Furthermore, it is becoming irritating when we see people who would spend 50 percent of their working hours looking at their phones – texting someone, reading e-mails, or checking social media feeds. It is more irritating when you invite friends to dinner and they cannot separate themselves from these phones, thinking perhaps that the sky will collapse if, God forbid, they miss something that everyone else is seeing, talking or laughing about.

Please, stop this nonsense; the world can survive a couple hours without you, at least until you finish your visit with friends. If you are able to do that, you would prove that you are the master, rather than the servant, of technology.

One of the many risks of being over-connected is that we start to pay attention to the thoughts and opinions of other people at the expense of those who are with us in the same room. Reality, then, would be over there instead of over here, and life becomes more distracted than focused. When one is always in a performance mood to keep up with the latest, one forgets how to be alone and relaxed. This is intoxicating, whether we are aware of it or not.

Why in the world do we need to be in touch with everyone on earth at any time through a smart-phone? Why do we need to put in our pocket thousands of songs through an iPod? Why do we need to have access to any possible research or any latest news through a pocket device without even considering waiting until we reach the living room appliance?

The arrival of such machines that provide all the conveniences of speed, variety of choices, access to unlimited knowledge, and instant connections, is deeply affecting the way we think, the way we act, and the way we live. Little by little, step by step, the intimate personal partnership between humans and machines is making machines more powerful and humans less relevant. We are becoming machine-centered in our way of thinking and living – focused on continuously updating our equipments to better serve our pride and selfish comfort – rather than human-centered – focused on consistently developing and perfecting what makes us more human.

What a liberation! What a tyranny!

No matter how efficient and sophisticated it is, the machine has no heart. It certainly produces more, but it is incapable of appreciating the value of what it produces. It might combine words of prayer, but it does not worship. It does not recognize God, it aims to be god, and often with a great success.

Idol-worship does not consist only in praying to statues and stones. It also consists in celebrating the man-made achievement as a latest version of a visible god. What better illustration than technology for that purpose! Through technology one can feel so powerful that he or she can create a human being in a laboratory. If one can do that, one can do anything else. It is only a question of time. Therefore, who needs God since god is what we achieve and, consequently, the ones who perform these achievements?

Just put together the right data, and you have what you were trying to find or invent – your little god.

Google, tell me, who is my god?

Let us not forget that we are a collection of all sorts of things. Think about it. You might be a collection of a father who abandoned you when you were a five-year old child, plus a very loving and dedicated mother, plus an uncle who helped you to grow up. You might be a collection of teachers who left a big impact on you, plus some friends who had been, and still are, there for you, plus some other friends who have already left you. You might be a collection of some books that directed your thoughts, plus your literature degree, plus the music you listened to all these years. You might be a collection of the religious services you attended, plus the country and ethnic group you grew up in, plus the programs you watched on TV, plus all these things you looked at on the Internet and your e-mails and the strangers you contacted there, and, and, and…

If you are able to collect all these data in your life and put them all in this magic machine called a "computer," then, by clicking the right button, you ask, "Google, tell me, who is my god?" the machine will tell you: I am your god and there is no other god beside me. The machine will also tell you what is going to happen to you in five, ten, or fifty years from now. It will tell you what kind of sickness you are going to have and how you are going to die. It will give you all the statistics you want that your brain cannot compute or even comprehend. It will tell you what is going well with you and what is wrong with you. It will define for you what is good and what is bad.

Technology is perhaps the most impressive tool known to humankind. But it can also be, since the argument of the serpent of Eden, the greatest tempter to inflate the ego and transform it into a god. It has the potential of convincing us that we are the masters of our destiny and we have the power to determine what is good and what is bad. This is when we lose track of God and we become our own gods. Let us remember the story of the serpent.

> Now the serpent was more crafty than any other wild animal that the Lord God had made. He said to the woman, "Did God say, 'You shall not eat from any tree in the garden'?" The woman said to the serpent, "We may eat of the fruit of the trees in the garden; but God said, 'You shall not eat of the fruit of the tree that is in the middle of the garden, nor shall you touch it, or you shall die.'" But the serpent said to the woman, "You will not die, for God knows that when you eat of it your eyes will be opened, and you will be like God, knowing good and evil." (Genesis 3:1-5)

Oh! How powerful we feel sometimes! At the click of that button, we jump from here to there. We transcend the miles. We overlook the time zones. We visit the most sophisticated places and websites. We explore the unknown. We inspire and edify generations, and we can infect them and corrupt them. We can be an instrument of grace and peace. But we can also learn how to make a bomb and bomb the people we don't like. Knowingly or unknowingly, we determine what is good and what is bad. We play god. "You will be like God, knowing good and evil," said the serpent.

No matter how marvelous this machine is, it does not have the answers for our most fundamental questions such as: "What is the meaning of life?" "Where did we come from?" "Where are we going?" "What is the point of being here, in the first place?" "Is existence better than non-existence?" "Is life better than death?" "Is a life of integrity better than a life of hypocrisy?" "What do human rights mean?" "Why are human values, values?" and many more questions like these.

We may be worshiping the high-tech-god who sent us to the moon, helped us to create a life in the lab, computed to us the most sophisticated equations our brain cannot comprehend, connected us instantly with the furthest possible location on earth. But this high-tech-god can also be a destroyer of everything we know, if this god cannot tell us what the meaning of life is, and why a good character is better than a bad character.

Here, the story of Khawarizmy comes to mind. Khawarizmy (780-850) was an astronomer, geographer and founder of several branches and basic concepts of mathematics. He was known as the "father of algebra." The following paraphrased story was attributed to him. It was reported that Khawarizmy, as the story said, was asked about the worth of a human being. He answered: a person of character is worth one (1). If this person has beauty, add to this (1) zero (10). If this person has money, add another zero (100). If this person has good family and prestige, add another zero (1000). But if you drop the number (1) that is the character, you also drop the worth of that person, and you end up with the zeros that have no value on their own.

Technology may provide us with a more comfortable life and with a good living, but it is not able to explain to us the meaning of life and why we need to make a life rather than a living. It is about tools that help us to live better. It is not about ends that enslave us and make us less human. It should be an addition to who we are, and not a definition of who we are.

Technology's advances should be matched with our increasing maturity and human development. Otherwise we may run the risk of slipping into making of technology, a god, rather than saying a prayer of praise and thanksgiving to the God of technology.

Conclusion

In Pursuit of an Unknown God

I must have been an "atheist" without knowing it. I do not believe in God – the god I was told about and I thought I used to know. I worship neither that God we crafted to fit our imagination and needs, nor the one whose temple is beautiful and gorgeous on the outside and shallow and worthless on the inside. I now have decided to join those whose altar carries the inscription, "To an unknown God" (Acts 17:23). This is what Saint Paul preached to the Athenians who had, beside many objects of worship, an altar for the unknown god. Paul, then, seized the opportunity to preach about the unknown God of that altar – the true God.

This "unknown God" is alive and active, and will never die, while the god we have created and pretended to have known for a long time died. Confirming his death, Friedrich Nietzsche declared: "God is dead."

Thank God; this is what such a god was supposed to do – die.

Civilization operates now according to secular principles. A war has been waged on religious faith, and religious people are supposed to keep their religion in the "closet." Now, the need for redefining religion and ethics without God seems to have become a priority. Very often we do this in a very cunning, soft, and suggestive strategy – the way of the serpent: "Did God really tell you…?" (Genesis 3:1 NAB). Anyway, God has died. We killed him for good, we thought, knowing that such a God has run its course in human history, and it is time for him to die.

But no; the reality is that we just replaced him – we replaced him with many gods. It is true that we no longer believe in Zeus, Apollo, and Neptune; we now believe in many gods, many goods, and many moralities. The old polytheism became the today relativism.

We no longer worship golden calves, we now worship money, power, pleasure, prestige, addictions, parties, ideologies, gurus, celebrities, sports, guns, careers, and weapons. We also worship obsessions with things such as Facebook, Twitter, video games, being thin, and many other things; every time we worship something, a new god is born. We used to have a place for worship at the center of town. Now we have banks, stores, restaurants, and some kinds of symbols for a promethean human achievement.

In fact, we worship the Promethean spirit in us, that is, the human person as the new god who is the origin of values, the maker of what is right and what is wrong, and the giver of the law rather than the receiver of it. We became our own gods by worshiping who we are and what we have done.

No matter what we call the god we crafted and we are now worshiping, if "he" is not defined as "God is love" (1 John 4:16), "he" is not only worthy of our worship, but "he" should die immediately in the same way the "old" god has died.

In the very essence of God's definition, there is this extraordinary force that can be called "interconnectedness," "bond,""relationship," "link," "connection," "tie," "union," or as Thich Nhat Hanh said, "inter-being." This kind of interaction that is part of our DNA cannot be isolated and labeled. It is something that is dynamic, experienced, and practical. It permeates reality as it is – favorable or not, messy or not, and dysfunctional or not. Love cannot be reduced to an abstract concept. Love is incarnational. Love must transform reality. Love is the greatest power known to humankind.

This is the miracle of unconditional love. With unconditional love come peace, justice, respect for others, care for those in need, significance, and a life worth living. There is no way such an unconditional love can be transformed into acts of terrorism, persecution, discrimination, and elimination of the other, especially when every "other" is part of one's "inter-being." Who am I without the other and who is the other without me? Love looks for everyone's special gifts to create greater unity in the world." God is love" and we are created in his image.

But why it is so difficult to find this God of love? Why it is much easier to find the god that is not God? Why do we prefer the god of "religion" to the religion of God? Why it is easier to follow a religion without God? What difference does our belief in God make? What difference does it make whether God exists or not? Why we are attracted to worship in the temples of our gods rather than in the temple that carries the inscription, "To an unknown God" (Acts 17:23) even though we know who he is – "God is love" (1 John 4:16)?

To such questions and to many more, this book has tried to provide an answer. It also tried to explain why religion, when it is reduced to an abstract concept or to the solely embodiment of human institutions, will not help men and women to achieve their life purpose and reach their highest potential and destiny. Instead, it may even be dangerous. A deformed religion – a religion with a false god or without god at all – could become no less than a weapon of mass destruction.

Religion is supposed to do just the opposite. It is supposed to be the way of mass construction by building the individual, the community, and the world. It will do that when it is the search for the true God and for his presence in our lives and in the world – a presence that transforms all things into divine. We do that by sticking with the very definition of God – "God is love." That is why Saint Paul was unyielding with his prescription for achieving this goal. He wrote about love the most inspiring words of all history. He said:

> And I will show you a still more excellent way. If I speak in the tongues of mortals and of angels, but do not have love, I am a noisy gong or a clanging cymbal. And if I have prophetic

powers, and understand all mysteries and all knowledge, and if I have all faith, so as to remove mountains, but do not have love, I am nothing. If I give away all my possessions, and if I hand over my body so that I may boast, but do not have love, I am nothing. Love is patient; love is kind; love is not envious or boastful or arrogant or rude. It does not insist on its own way; it is not irritable or resentful; it does not rejoice in wrongdoing, but rejoices in the truth. It bears all things, believes all things, hopes all things, endures all things. Love never ends. (1 Corinthians 13:1-8)

The way of love is by far more demanding than the righteousness and literalism of a dogmatic and institutional religion. That is why Saint Augustine dared to say: *"Ama et fac quod vis"* (Love and do what you will). He knew that what we would do, when we have the love of God in our hearts, was good precisely because it would be necessarily inspired by God's love. The God of love died for our love. We should die for his love too. This is the message we need today, more than ever.

Of course we still need to abide by the institutions, the religious traditions, the rules, and the instructions of the legitimate authority. Our responsibility is to make sure that all of our human structures are based on what God has revealed – God is greater than any social constitution and any subjective endeavor. However, we should do all this with the eyes of love. It is not the application of the law per se that will save us, it is rather the love that inspires and transforms everything we do into pathways for salvation. To put it more bluntly, religion is the way of salvation when love animates it; without love, the "perfect" observance of the rituals and regulations remains by itself an empty posture. No wonder Teilhard de Chardin asked a formidable question whose consequences are enormous and very grave. He asked: "(…) [Is] it not a fact, as I can warrant, that if the love of God were extinguished in the souls of the faithful, the enormous edifice of rites, of hierarchy and of doctrines that comprise the Church would instantly revert to the dust from which it rose?"Martin Luther King, Jr. said: "Love is the only force capable of transforming an enemy into a friend."

Also it is appropriate to mention that if performing loving things is important, being a loving person is much more important. We can perform loving things out of philanthropy or for self-interest and satisfactory reasons, but when we become loving persons we do things with God's hands and according to God's perception. This means, then, that the people we used to consider as irritant and enemies are actually facets of God's face. Doesn't this change every relationship we have?

Religion, without love, will rather distance us from God and from the sacred. But religion, with love, will be the most certain way that leads to God and the sacred. Religion is the hearth. Love is the fire. God's love makes us loving and lovable. "Love," wrote Teilhard de Chardin, "is the most universal, formidable and mysterious of cosmic energies…. Could it not be, in essence, the attraction which is exercised upon each conscious element by the center of the universe?"

"God is love," indeed. Love is the actual form of God. This God did not, and will not, die. In fact, he should be in charge because if he dies, the promethean man will also die. Don't we have signs of that? Our culture is starting to be more aware of its limitations. By trying to act as God did not exist, by replacing him with the promethean man as the center of the universe, by strictly separating the temporal from the spiritual, and by having faith in reason, science, and progress, rather than in God and his law, we are realizing that the world we dreamed of is not the one we are seeing at the present time. Although this culture has reached a high degree of marvelous achievements, it also poisoned our lives by providing and exporting violence through books, films, magazines, video games, weapons, and more weapons. In such a case, why, in the world, we are shocked if this violence that we provided returned to us to make us victims, and with the atrocity that sent us back to the primitive Stone Age? What has happened to what we have proudly called "civilization," "progress," and "human rights"? What has happened to the promethean man? What has happened to the liberated individual that was prophesied, "Ah, you who call evil good and good evil, who put darkness for light and light for darkness, who put bitter for sweet and sweet for bitter! Ah, you who are wise in your own eyes, and shrewd in your own sight!" (Isaiah 5:20-21)? What has happened to the "wise" of this world who rejected the well proven advice, "Trust the Lord with all your heart, and do not rely on your own insight. In all your ways acknowledge him, and he will make straight your paths. Do not be wise in your own eyes; fear the Lord, and turn away from evil. It will be a healing for your flesh and a refreshment for your body" (Proverbs 3:5-8)?

There is no guarantee for the promethean man to survive if God is ousted. They will "survive" together or they will "die" together. Therefore, nothing is more important than finding God – the God of love. Pedro Arrupe put it so beautifully this way:

Nothing is more practical than finding God, that is, than falling in love in a quite absolute, final way. What you are in love with, what seizes your imagination, will affect everything. It will decide what will get you out of bed in the morning, what you will do with your evenings, how you spend your weekends, what you read, who you know, what breaks your heart, and what amazes you with joy and gratitude. Fall in love, stay in love, and it will decide everything.

For, as Mahatma Gandhi observed, "Where love is, there God is also."

About the Author

Dr. Jean Maalouf's books (more than 50 books and essays) have been published in the United States of America, Canada, Mexico, Colombia, France, Spain, Portugal, Philippines, and India. Also, he has written many articles on topics of religion, spirituality, mysticism (Eastern and Western), philosophy, psychology, and peace and social issues for journals and magazines such as *Catholic Digest, Celebration, National Herald* (New Delhi), *Peace Research Reviews* (Canada), *Praying, Revue des Sciences Philosophiques et Théologiques* (Paris), *Spirit & Life, Spiritual Life, Teilhard Perspective.* He is a member of several professional associations that include American Academy of Religion, American Teilhard Association, Association des Amis de P. Teilhard de Chardin (Paris), The Authors Guild, Contemplative Outreach, Centering Prayer, National Writers Union, Fellowship of Catholic Scholars, Catholic Writers Guild, and The Society of Christian Philosophers.

The messages in Dr. Maalouf's writings seem deeply personal as if they were written just for the person who is reading them, and yet, they are timeless and universal. His works were hailed by critics with terms such as these: "Jean Maalouf brings his experience as doctor of philosophy and humanities to bear in works of spirituality. His focus is one of gentle revolution in human development," "Maalouf has written in the style of Meister Eckhart, John of the Cross, and St. Irenaeus," "Maalouf's gift for writing about the most sublime truths in the most simple language allows him... to touch and transform the hearts of believers and non-believers alike." He is blessed with the art of provoking thoughts that inspire new choices, influence decisions, and get the attention of both the religious and secular worlds, as well as the academic and the non-academic ones. In a culture that often relegates God to loftiness, he knows how to provide compelling images of God in unexpected places—in the most ordinary stuff of our daily lives. It is no wonder then, that he sees, because of the continuous Incarnation in everyday life, how one can transform his or her daily life through moments of grace in life.

Also by Dr. Jean Maalouf

Publications in English

Awakening to the Philosophy of Jesus

Bold Prayers from the Heart

The Burning Flame of Love

Change Your World: Awakening to the Power of Truth – Beauty – Simplicity - Change

Christmas Shock: The Human Experience of God

The Divine Milieu: A Spiritual Classic for Today and Tomorrow (Essay)

Experiencing Jesus with Mother Teresa

Fully Alive: God's Prescription for a Happier and Healthier Life

Heal Your Life: awakening to the Power of Faith – Hope – Love - Prayer

The Healing Power of Beauty

The Healing Power of Change

The Healing Power of Faith

The Healing Power of Forgiveness

The Healing Power of Friendship

The Healing Power of Gratitude

The Healing Power of Hope

The Healing Power of Joy

The Healing Power of Kindness

The Healing Power of Love

The Healing Power of Peace

The Healing Power of Prayer

The Healing Power of Purpose

The Healing Power of Simplicity

The Healing Power of Truth

I Can Tell God Anything: Living Prayer

If We Just See What They See: Peace According to Albert Einstein, Thomas Merton, Pope John XXIII, Thich Nhat Hanh, Mahatma Gandhi, Teilhard de Chardin, Mother Teresa of Calcutta

Intimacies: The Miracle of Love

I've Got One Life to Live: Radiant Health God's Way

Jesus Laughed and Other Reflections on Being Human

The Little Way: Fresh Air for the Soul — A Retreat with Saint Thérèse of Lisieux

Live a Life That Matters: Awakening to the Power of Purpose — Kindness — Forgiveness -- Friendship

Making All Things New

Mother Teresa: Essential Writings (Editor)

Pathways: Finding God in the Present Moment

Pope John XXIII: Essential Writings (Editor)

Practicing the Presence of the Living God: A Retreat with Brother Lawrence of the Resurrection

Praying with Mother Teresa

Teilhard and the Feminine (Essay)

Teilhard de Chardin: Reconciliation in Christ (Editor)

Teilhard's Proposition for Peace: Rediscovering the Fire

Touch a Single Leaf: Teilhard and Peace

Touchstones for Peace (Essay)

Transformation in Prayer: 99 Sayings by M. Basil Pennington (Editor)

Where Has God Gone?

Your New Adventure: Make the Most of the Rest of Your Life

Contributor to:

> *Encyclopedia of Catholic Social Thought, Social Science, and Social Policy*

Publications in French

Le Mystère du Mal dans L'Oeuvre de Teilhard de Chardin

Teilhard de Chardin et le mystère du mal. Evolutionisme? Stoïcisme? Christocentrisme? (Essay)

Le Réenchantement du Monde (Co-author)

La Terre Est Mon Pays (Co-author)

Publications in Spanish (Translated from English)

Dile a Dios Lo Que Sientes: Oración Desde La Vida

El Poder Sanador De La Alegría

El Poder Sanador De La Amistad

El Poder Sanador De La Bondad

El Poder Sanador De La Esperanza

El Poder Sanador De La Fe

El Poder Sanador De La Oración

El Poder Sanador Del Amor

El Poder Sanador De La Paz

El Poder Sanador Del Perdón

El Poder Sanador De Tener Un Propósito

Juan XXIII: Escritos Esenciales

Madre Teresa de Calcuta: Escritos Esenciales Orando
Con La Madre Teresa
Orando Con La Madre Teresa De Calcuta

Publications in Portuguese (Translated from English)

O Poder Da Cura Pela Alegria
O Poder Da Cura Pela Amizade
O Poder Da Cura Pela Amor
O Poder Da Cura Pela Paz